Mixed Intelligent Systems

Tadeusz A. Grzeszczyk

Mixed Intelligent Systems

Developing Models for Project Management and
Evaluation

Tadeusz A. Grzeszczyk
Warsaw University of Technology
Warsaw, Poland

ISBN 978-3-319-91157-1   ISBN 978-3-319-91158-8   (eBook)
https://doi.org/10.1007/978-3-319-91158-8

Library of Congress Control Number: 2018942134

Cover illustration: Modern building window © saulgranda/Getty

Printed on acid-free paper

This Palgrave Pivot imprint is published by the registered company Springer International Publishing AG part of Springer Nature.
The registered company address is: Gewerbestrasse 11, 6330 Cham, Switzerland

CONTENTS

LIST OF FIGURES

LIST OF TABLES

CHAPTER 1

Introduction

Abstract The origin of this book is the result of identifying the need and the opportunity to continue conducting interdisciplinary research concerning the development of new models of comprehensive project evaluation systems. Since evaluation systems should have a multidimensional and comprehensive nature, one ought to use different methods and systems to ensure the integration of quantitative and qualitative criteria. The introductory chapter contains a brief presentation of underlying assumptions, the undertaken study, the main research objective, which is the study regarding the needs and possibilities of using mixed intelligent systems in project management and evaluation, along with selecting model solutions in this area. Moreover, it also roughly provides justification for the increasing importance of systemic and interdisciplinary research in the field of evaluation, as well as outlines the structure of the book.

Keywords Interdisciplinary research in evaluation • Traditional and intelligent systems • Mixed methods and systems

This book is dedicated to mixed (integrated, hybrid, combined) intelligent systems for project evaluation and indicates contemporary challenges resulting from the current state of knowledge in the fields of mixed methods studies, knowledge engineering, Artificial Intelligence (AI), project management, and evaluation based on business and management sciences. Dealing with this kind of research problem is justified by thinking about

© The Author(s) 2018
T. A. Grzeszczyk, *Mixed Intelligent Systems*,
https://doi.org/10.1007/978-3-319-91158-8_1

1

the further development of theory and practical achievements in research concerning intelligent systems for project evaluation.

The origin of this book is the result of identifying the need and the opportunity to continue conducting interdisciplinary research concerning the development of new models of comprehensive project evaluation systems. The correct functioning of evaluation systems directly influences the efficient and effective planning and implementation of various types of project and organizational achievement objectives. Projects, in fact, play an increasingly important role in realizing the goals of modern business and non-commercial organizations, where both the projects and their evaluation processes are complex, unique and have a multifaceted nature.

Since evaluation systems should have a multidimensional and comprehensive nature, one ought to use different methods and systems to ensure the integration of quantitative and qualitative criteria. There are no simple answers to research questions concerning the correctness and value of contemporary projects; no single method, system or approach can decipher the inherent complexities, and several quantitative and qualitative methods, used simultaneously, are needed (American Evaluation Association 2009). Mixing and matching methods and systems in evaluation procedures is a rule rather than an exception (Williams 1999).

In the most popular definition, mixed methods research is a process of integration of both qualitative and quantitative methods and systems of data collection and analysis in order to better understand research goals (Plano Clark and Ivankova 2015). Studies conducted demonstrate that the use of mixed methods research together with quantitative and qualitative approaches in research processes leads to the creation of a more holistic image of multifaceted research than conventional analytical methods (Brannen 2005). This is particularly desirable in complex evaluation studies. The increased demand for mixed evaluation methods can be illustrated by the raising of awareness among evaluators concerning complexity issues and, therefore, the rapid increase in interest in this topic (Mertens 2017). The popularity of mixed research is evident through the formation of special interest groups, professional associations, the production of journal articles, books and conference papers, and the use of the terms 'third methodological movement', 'third research paradigm' and 'new star in the social science sky' (Creswell and Plano Clark 2017).

Mixing various evaluation methods and systems represents one of the alternative directions of project evaluation systems in their development toward complex and comprehensive solutions. Models based on several methods and systems can improve the quality of evaluation results and lead to more objective research. Therefore, studies related to the search for new models that contribute to the improvement of previously known evaluation systems and combine several methods are justified. In particular, it may be useful to combine project evaluation models that utilize both traditional evaluation systems and systems based on AI and knowledge engineering (Grzeszczyk 2013).

There is a need to conduct interdisciplinary research, beyond conventional academic boundaries, within combined models from several scientific disciplines and to use a variety of methods and systems applications in solving complex project evaluation problems. This type of approach is in line with the interdisciplinary nature of the comprehensive project evaluation problem and refers to the increasingly popular idea of science without borders. One should use many academic disciplinary approaches to solve project evaluation problems, drawing on business, management and social sciences. Within the framework of interdisciplinary methodological research, there is a need to investigate methods known within several established disciplines used for the modeling and implementation of mixed intelligent systems for project evaluation.

The key assumptions underlying the research presented are as follows:

1. Interdisciplinary study, conducted on the basis of business and management sciences, concerning the development of new models of comprehensive project evaluation systems and the combined use of several methods, including both hard and soft methodologies, allows for multidimensional research perspectives and reduces the disadvantages of methods and systems used separately.
2. Intelligent and classical systems of decision-making, systems approaches, Integral Theory and innovative technologies based on AI and Knowledge Engineering as new factors within project management research can lead to significant opportunities for the development of new, comprehensive project evaluation systems.

The potential development of models for project management and evaluation can be enhanced by the continuous verification and enrichment of the degree of differentiation of methods and systems as well as their improvement, in order to increase the accuracy of decisions taken. Application of AI and knowledge engineering systems, in addition to classic solutions, in integrated systems justifies the use of the term 'mixed intelligent systems'.

The main research objective of this study is to investigate the needs and possibilities of using mixed intelligent systems in project management and evaluation and also to propose selected model solutions in this area.

The structure of the book results from the key assumptions and main objective of this scientific research. The book consists of seven chapters. After the introduction, Chap. 2 presents basic issues related to project evaluation. Chapter 3 deals with quantitative evaluation methods while Chap. 4 focuses on qualitative methods. Selected problems that concern systems integrating quantitative and qualitative methods and systems are discussed in Chap. 5. Considerations related to the process of modeling mixed intelligent systems are presented in the penultimate chapter (Chap. 6). These studies allow the formulation of a final summary and recommendations in line with the research objective and the results achieved.

References

American Evaluation Association. (2009). *An Evaluation Roadmap for a More Effective Government.*

Brannen, J. (2005). Mixing Methods: The Entry of Qualitative and Quantitative Approaches into the Research Process. *International Journal of Social Research Methodology, 8*(3): 173–184.

Creswell, J. W., & Plano Clark, V. L. (2017). *Designing and Conducting Mixed Methods Research.* California: SAGE Publications Inc. Thousand Oaks California 91320.

Grzeszczyk, T. A. (2013). *Towards the Model of Comprehensive Project Evaluation System.* Warsaw: Faculty of Management, Warsaw University of Technology.

Mertens, D. M. (2017). *Mixed Methods Design in Evaluation.* California: SAGE Publications Inc. Thousand Oaks California 91320.

Plano Clark, V. L., & Ivankova, N. V. (2015). *Mixed Methods Research: A Guide to the Field.* California: SAGE Publications Inc. Thousand Oaks California 91320.

Williams, K. (1999). *Mixing Quantitative and Qualitative Evaluation Tools: A Pragmatic Approach.* Lyon: The Centre for European Evaluation Expertise – C3E.

CHAPTER 2

Basic Aspects Related to Project Evaluation

Abstract This chapter focuses on basic aspects related to project evaluation. The author begins by introducing selected terminology used throughout the book. Since project evaluation is a complex issue, additional attention is drawn to various project evaluation criteria. The necessity of basing an evaluation process on various evaluation criteria results from the complexity and multifacetedness of the evaluation problems connected with many kinds of project. Next, the chapter addresses the systems, methods, techniques and tools used both in project evaluation and in comprehensive evaluation systems. The author also offers some insight into AI systems used in comprehensive evaluation. AI methods are an essential complement to classical methods, because they may be used to solve decision problems under uncertainty conditions. The chapter concludes with a comparison of quantitative versus qualitative methods, leading to an in-depth analysis in the subsequent chapters.

Keywords Project management • Project evaluation • Quantitative and qualitative evaluation • Evaluation and monitoring systems • Comprehensive evaluation systems

© The Author(s) 2018
T. A. Grzeszczyk, *Mixed Intelligent Systems*,
https://doi.org/10.1007/978-3-319-91158-8_2

2.1   TERMINOLOGY ISSUES

It is necessary to provide a comprehensive presentation concerning the essence of the most important concepts used in this book. The basis for the terminology analysis is selected developments in the business and management disciplines, included within the social sciences. The concepts analysis and considerations about terminology issues relate primarily to the following terms: project, project management, evaluation, project evaluation, project evaluation system, evaluation and monitoring systems, intelligent systems and mixed intelligent systems.

The first term 'project' and other directly related concepts should be explained. A project means activities with an assumed time duration, undertaken to complete objectives by creating some unique (tangible or intangible) product, service, result or a combination of these (PMBOK Guide 2017). The main project constraints are costs, schedule, scope, resources and quality.

A set of smaller, interrelated projects implemented to achieve common major strategic objectives constitutes a large program. Sometimes, individual large and complex projects are called programs, to emphasize their complexity, size and importance. 'Project portfolio' usually refers to a set of projects, investments or programs, whose consolidated objective is to help achieve the financial and strategic goals of the organization, under constrained resource conditions (Bayney and Chakravarti 2012).

In this case, a collection of related and independent work or projects may create an organizational portfolio that is built to achieve benefits consistent with the purposes of high-level business strategic plans. Generally, programs and portfolios are understood as something more complex than single projects.

The 'project' is also related to the 'project family' concept, which refers to projects associated with a cause-effect relationship of the ancestor-descendant type. Such understanding of this concept usually means that outputs, outcomes and impacts of previously completed projects are applied, to define the projects which follow them (Gasik 2015).

Project management might be defined as the processes of planning, scheduling and controlling of the action sequence leading to the effective and efficient implementation of the objectives expected by the project stakeholders—individuals or organizations involved in the project, or affected by the project activity or outcomes (Kerzner 2004). Projects which form a program are usually managed together, but some projects and work which constitute a portfolio might not be interrelated. In the case of a project family, a manager aggregates the results achieved by each project separately and the results attained should contribute to the organization's strategy.

A project, program, portfolio, family, policy, strategy, process, system, initiative, action or product, among other aspects, can be evaluated. The 'evaluation' concept is related to a variety of terms: assessment, appraisal, analysis, testing, criticism, supervision, scrutiny, study, research, grading, examination, inspection, judgment, ranking, review and control. These concepts cannot be treated as synonyms of evaluation. For example, the term 'appraisal' is used in the case of a preliminary project evaluation (ex-ante project evaluation). In turn, 'judgment' can be understood as the final element of a comprehensive evaluation process. The 'assessment' concept has a narrower meaning. In educational programs, assessment applies to individual students, and evaluation concerns the quality or value of projects, programs and policies (Wang 2017). Different types of assessment may be appropriate to various aspects of evaluation, for example, need for the project, project design, project logic (theory), cost and efficiency, outcomes and impact (Rossi et al. 2004).

In the best-known definition, evaluation is the product of the systematic process of determining the merit, worth or value of an object (Scriven 1991). Patton, in his definition, focused on outcomes in addition to project and program improvement. Evaluation is the process of systematic gathering of both quantitative and qualitative data: information as well as knowledge about the activities, features and outcomes (results) of projects or programs, in order to make judgments about these evaluation objects, increase understanding and knowledge, improve or further develop project or program effectiveness and efficiency, support decisions concerning future programming and/or raise understanding (Patton 2015).

Evaluation of outcomes should be distinguished from outcomes measurement that has a narrower sense. Outcomes measurement concerns only quantitative outcomes indicators, in contrast to outcomes evaluation which refers to any quantitative and qualitative data. Utilization-focused project and program evaluation is conducted with particular intended uses in mind (Patton 2015).

The issues concerning the comprehensive modeling of contemporary project evaluation are often complex interdisciplinary problems and it is necessary to apply systems thinking approaches to solve them. Therefore, another important term used in this book is 'project evaluation system'.

Evaluation systems are used for the estimation of the project value, taking into account the previously stated purpose, principles and methods (classical and AI methods), which should be calculated based on the information and knowledge collected and analyzed for this purpose (Grzeszczyk 2012).

The issue of building different artificial intelligence models for a comprehensive project evaluation system is among the problems concerning the use of new Information and Communication Technologies (ICT), which allow the implementation of modern computational intelligence systems (intelligent systems) for the analysis of complex, multifaceted and multidisciplinary, socio-economic evaluation problems.

Project evaluation systems can by classified according to various criteria (evaluation time, unit, objective and subject), among which the most popular is the time criterion (before, during and after project implementation), as well as the typology connected with the project or program life cycle. According to the Project Management Institute (PMI), the program life cycle consists of the following phases connected with a program: preparation, initiation, setup, benefits delivery and closure (Sanderson 2012).

The cycle of operations, according to Project Cycle Management (PCM) methodology has five successive phases repeated iteratively: programming, identification, formulation, implementation (including monitoring and reporting), followed by final evaluation and audit (Aid Delivery Methods 2014). In connection with PCM, project evaluation systems can be divided into the following: ex-ante evaluation (appraisal), ongoing evaluation, ex-post evaluation and long-term impact evaluation.

Ex-ante evaluation (aka appraisal, forward-looking evaluation) systems play an important role in the process of project proposal planning and refer to the period before starting project implementation (looking ahead into the future and prognostic research). Ongoing (in-vivo) evaluation systems relate to selected moments during project implementation and facilitates project modification through its realization and investigating activities, compared with ex-ante evaluation reports, which support monitoring system functioning and the preparation of final evaluation systems. Similar to the ongoing evaluation concept is mid-term evaluation, but this is carried out less frequently, that is, halfway through project implementation. After finishing projects and achieving their short-term objectives, an ex-post evaluation (aka final, completion evaluation, end-of-project) system is used. Long-term impact evaluation is conducted, in order to investigate broader changes and project long-term effects (resulting from program outcomes) taking place within organizations, regions, societies or environments. Analysis is subject to both positive (planned) impacts and negative long-term effects, previously unexpected. Ex-post evaluation and long-term impact evaluation are useful for ex-ante evaluation and previous ongoing evaluation verifications.

There are two other important concepts associated with the aforementioned types of evaluation: summative and formative evaluations (Fig. 2.1). Summative evaluation deals with judging the merit of fixed, unchanging, completed projects as a finished product, in contrast to formative evaluation which is an ongoing evaluation, not fixed but used to improve interventions and still in the process of change (Little 2013).

In addition to the project evaluation system, there are also project monitoring, control and auditing systems. These are different concepts requiring terminology explanations. The most frequent research areas of evaluation concern more complex issues, such as the logical structure of the activities of the project and the long-term effects and impact. A project evaluation system should incorporate knowledge management, learning processes implementation and the improvement of the current project and should generate knowledge useful for future projects. Monitoring should operate simultaneously with the entire project and measure short-term indicators—regarding project resources, activities and measurable objectives (Chen 2004). The implementation of this continuous monitoring

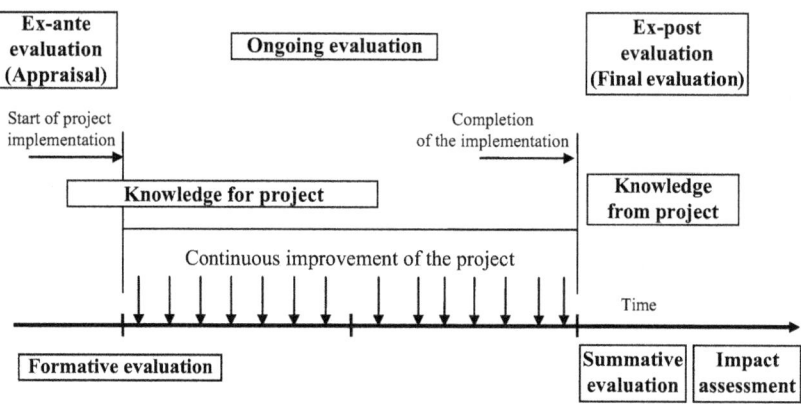

Fig. 2.1 Types of evaluation. (Source: Based on Grzeszczyk (2013a))

process allows the conducting of ongoing activities for tracking project progress and the identification of emerging imperfections, irregularities and errors.

In parallel with monitoring, current control (inspection) is often supported and performed. Control is also conducted after a project's completion, at random (sample check), and usually refers to the financial and legal aspects of organizations implementing projects.

Audit systems can support financial control and sometimes these two terms are used interchangeably. Audit assesses, among other aspects, the legality, economy, equity, fairness, transparency and openness of the institution, which is stated in the public finance act and can support evaluation systems in terms of financial and legal issues, when auditors identify control points and the components of financial statements (Gray and Manson 2011).

A project audit should be implemented in accordance with formal recommendations and auditing standards during the project realization, after the end of a particular project realization stage or only after completion of the entire project. In particular, the audit objectives are assessing project management quality, the efficiency of applied project management tools, the quality and purposefulness of project documentation, accordance of achieved project outputs with planned outputs, as well as project objectives (Project Audit Methodology 2018).

At the end of this section, 'intelligent systems' and 'mixed (integrated, hybrid, combined) intelligent systems' terminology will be outlined, since these play a fundamental role in this book's considerations. Mixing may be characterized as connecting several objects and subsystems into one efficient and effective system that works better than the individual subsystems separately. Mixed intelligent systems for project evaluation can be based on classical methods (e.g. statistical, logic models, expert panels) and AI techniques, such as neural networks, rule-based systems, evolutionary computation (e.g. genetic algorithms), case-based reasoning, rough or fuzzy systems and others.

2.2   Project Evaluation Criteria

Systematic evaluation research uses assumed evaluation criteria to develop, improve or better understand the evaluated project (Rossi et al. 2004). The necessity for basing this on various evaluation criteria in the evaluation process results from the complexity and multifacetedness of the evaluation problems connected with many kinds of project. Such criteria support the forming of evaluation questions and outline the objective range of evaluation processes, and thereby the evaluation problems which are to be solved.

The evaluation criteria should be selected depending on the research problems and the evaluation type that is (Wholey et al. 2010):

- ex-ante, ongoing, ex-post or long-term impact evaluation,
- one-shot or ongoing,
- commercial or public,
- existing or designed criteria,
- quantitative, qualitative or mixed,
- formative or summative,
- goal-based or goal-free,
- problem orientation or non-problem,
- objective observer or participatory.

Some pre-evaluation activity (such as evaluability assessment) may be helpful in the process of selecting evaluation criteria and support the assessment of the project's readiness for evaluation. Evaluability assessment supports the reaching agreement with key stakeholders regarding realistic project objectives, measures of project performance and the selection of appropriate evaluation criteria (Wholey et al. 2010).

There are a number of systems supporting the determination of a suitable choice of criteria and principles for judging realistic project objectives measures and indicators, which are based on SMART (Specific, Measurable, Achievable, Relevant, Trackable), SPICED (Subjective, Participatory, Interpretable, Cross-checked, Empowering, Disaggregated) (Green and South 2006), CREAM (Clear, Relevant, Economic, Adequate, Monitorable) (Schiavo-Campo and Tommasi 1999) and other approaches (Lopez-Acevedo et al. 2012).

The standard understanding of 'SMART criteria' for judging project goals and objectives is that criteria should meet the following five requirements: 'specific' (unambiguous defining of what is to be measured), 'measurable' (offers the possibility of presenting evaluation results in a numerical form), 'achievable' and 'agreed', 'relevant' (real premises which are possible to achieve) as well as trackable and time-specific (able to be identified and measured within a time scale). Understanding SPICED and CREAM requirements follows similar criteria.

On the basis of correctly formulated project goals, objectives and evaluation criteria, the creation of evaluation questions takes place. Answers to these questions should be included in the final evaluation report. The basic set of evaluation criteria is as follows: efficiency, effectiveness, relevance, sustainability and impact. The essence of the three levels of evaluation and the principles of understanding its criteria is presented in Figs. 2.2 and 2.3.

Efficiency defines project economy, is used to examine the way external resources transform into products, outcomes (results) and impacts, and is determined by comparison of cost and benefits. Effectiveness concentrates only on products, outcomes (results) and impacts, without taking costs and other input resources into account. Relevance, and a similar criterion, usefulness, concern the study of the conformity of project objectives with existing and dynamically changing socio-economic needs and problems in specific areas affected by the project.

Sustainability (utility) relates to the study of a conformity degree of long-term interactions of implemented projects with the real local and regional needs of particular target groups. The research involves the iden-

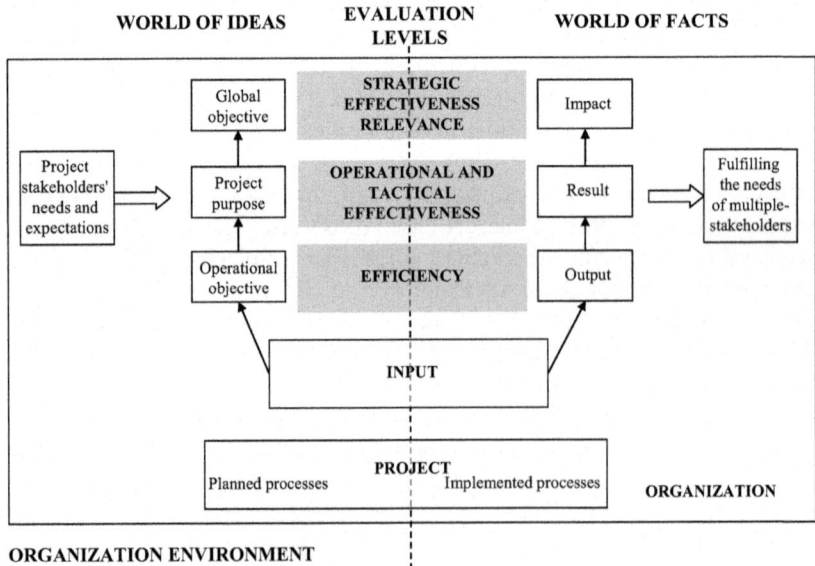

Fig. 2.2   Three levels of evaluation. (Source: Based on Trocki (2012) and Gudda (2011))

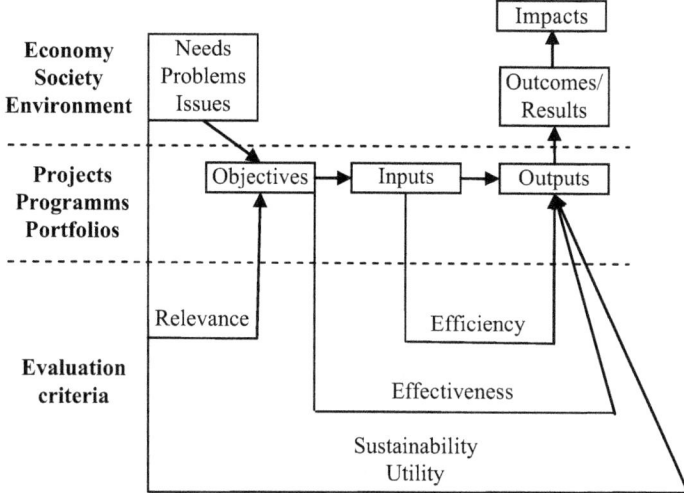

Fig. 2.3 Understanding of key evaluation criteria. (Source: Based on The New Programming Period (2006))

tification of required permanent changes achieved in the areas of evaluated project impacts, a relatively long time after completion of the planned project activities.

The criteria mentioned in this section have been popularized in relation to the dissemination of knowledge regarding the evaluation of European and public projects. It is not a closed and finite set of applied criteria. Depending on the specificity of the projects evaluated, additional criteria might be added, for example, referring to social, economic, environmental, technological, scientific and other aspects.

2.3   Systems, Methods, Techniques and Tools in Project Evaluation

The suitable choice of evaluation approaches, systems, methods, techniques and tools is among the most important aspects connected with the preparation and execution of project evaluation. 'Approach' is the most general term, which usually indicates the theoretical basis of fundamental considerations and helps determine the general assumptions and principles useful within the processes of designing systems, models, methods, techniques or tools.

In project management systems, approaches play a fundamental role, and it is necessary to use this type of approach in project evaluation processes, which should be implemented in an orderly and systematic way. Two major perspectives that enable the distinguishing of differences between systems approaches are 'thinking about systems' and 'systems thinking' (Reynolds and Holwell 2010).

Project evaluation can be considered as a system of action that consists of elements connected with a causal (cause-effect) relationship. Elements of this system are interrelated and create an organized set, relatively isolated from the environment. Individual elements perform separate functions in order to achieve the common goal of the whole system, which is the evaluation process realization, in a way consistent with earlier assumptions.

Individual elements perform separate functions in order to achieve the common goal of the whole system, which is the evaluation process implementation. This implementation should be in line with previously accepted theoretical and practical assumptions on which the evaluation models used are based.

In addition to evaluation systems, subsystems also exist within them (Fig. 2.4). An example of a system larger than the program evaluation system (a system in itself) might be the evaluation system of a corporate strategy or public policy system (in the case of development and public projects).

Evaluation is characterized by its interdisciplinary nature and is a process that requires the application of interdisciplinary methods, techniques,

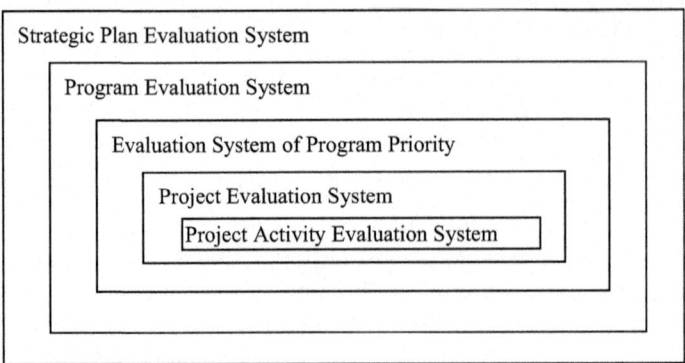

Fig. 2.4 Evaluation systems and subsystems

procedures and tools. Various research methods can be used to build a comprehensive system of evaluation methods (Grzeszczyk 2013b). The elements of this system are organized in accordance with certain stages of the evaluation process and it is often necessary to modify them iteratively, taking into account the specificity of the projects evaluated in each specific situation.

Methodologies and project evaluation methods are of key importance for the development of evaluation. Evaluation methodologies are a theoretical and systematic study, in accordance with selected paradigms, and concern principles, guidelines, general research assumptions about basic scientific evaluation methods known in various scientific disciplines. The following are features which serve to distinguish the scientific method from the non-scientific: objectivity, repeatability, rigor, purposiveness, economic viability, generalizability, testability, confidence and precision (Krishnaswamy et al. 2009).

Methods in general are a way of acting that is justified scientifically, which means the conscious and repetitive choice of a specific action by researchers. Methods, in a detailed sense, define a set of purposeful activities, engaging resources to solve problems; thus it is a description of the way of reaching a desirable solution for this problem and is a result of execution of certain tasks.

A scientific method is a set of techniques, procedures and tools for investigating phenomena, supporting new knowledge, and discovering and correcting or integrating previous knowledge. They are used for collection of data through experimentation as well as observation, and in the next stage formulation as well as testing of hypotheses takes place on the basis of these data. In many cases it is necessary to use interdisciplinary approaches and methodological pluralism by using mixed methods systems (Gill et al. 2010).

Usually, highly diverse evaluation methods constitute important objects of complex multidimensional and interdisciplinary research methodology based on the social sciences. These methods should cover many aspects of projects, due to their complexity and unique character and may be classified in different ways; for example, quite a popular type of method typology involves the division into comprehensive and fragmentary methods which are often identified with techniques.

Comprehensive methods might include, among others, cost-benefit analysis, business case, cost-effectiveness analysis, feasibility study and specific methods established by several organizations because of their own needs. Various fragmentary methods can be assigned to different stages of a multi-stage evaluation process, within which can be distinguished, for example, the four stages: structuring, data collection, gathered data analysis and the research process results formulation.

Despite the fact that each evaluation process has a unique character resulting from the uniqueness of each project and the evaluator's intention, it is possible to design and implement an evaluation using a process approach. Such a repeatable process consists of a specified number of stages to which a range of fragmentary methods that are the elements of the evaluation system can be assigned.

Among fragmentary methods of the evaluation structuring process are, for example, SWOT analysis, LFM-based methods, the project logic model, Metaplan (shared understanding) and others. The most popular methods to help data collection include, for example, survey research, personal interview, drop and collect survey, qualitative research, secondary data-based methods and others. The third stage (gathered data analysis) uses, among other methods, various statistical analyses, econometric models, geographic information systems, shift analysis, comparative groups and new methods based on knowledge engineering and artificial intelligence approaches.

Methods for the last stage (research process results formulation) include, for example, multi-criteria expert-based analysis, statistical multi-criteria analysis, benchmarking, fragmentary cost-effectiveness analysis, fragmentary cost-benefit analysis and others.

Ancillary functions to systems and methods provide techniques and tools—the last of the concepts listed earlier at the beginning of this section. Systems, methods, techniques, procedures and tools used together in evaluation processes can be called research evaluation instruments. Evaluation techniques include, among others, investment projects evaluation techniques and monetary evaluation techniques, with the use of simple versions of financial indicators, weighted average scores and multi-criteria analysis.

Studies on the approaches, systems, methods, techniques, procedures and tools that can be useful in project evaluation should be conducted on an interdisciplinary basis, according to the complex systems theory. Continuing research is an opportunity to open up new areas of research on the enrichment of applied research evaluation instruments useful in both fragmentary evaluation and comprehensive processes.

2.4   COMPREHENSIVE AND COMPLEX EVALUATION SYSTEMS

Many projects are very difficult to evaluate and to subject to management risk analysis because of their highly complex forms, with multiple interdependencies. Complex and complicated projects necessitate a comprehensive evaluation, based on complex and comprehensive evaluation systems, which should take into account stakeholders with diverse and compound needs, various factors and complex multiple project relations (Xie and Yang 2011).

Therefore, in the context of evaluation, 'comprehensive' and 'complex' concepts are often used. Synonyms of the term 'comprehensive' are wide, extensive, broad and full, (www.dictionary.com 2017) and this term means dealing with all, or almost all aspects or elements of something (en.oxforddictionaries.com 2017). In turn, the concept 'complex' derives from the Latin word 'complexus' which means integrating many phenomena, factors and dimensions. The term 'comprehensive' usually refers to the type of methods and systems used in evaluation research, while complex projects are those that are subject to this research.

Comprehensive systems for project evaluation ought to be characterized by multidimensionality and multifaceted methods of integration, taking into consideration relationships between individual elements (managing knowledge about these elements) of the project, treated as a complex system, the collective behaviors of this whole system and its relationships with its environment. Shared elements and relationships between these are usually highly diverse, which causes complications in complex project evaluation.

A profitability evaluation of complex and multi-aspect projects can be carried out based on the various resources involved and a received benefits assessment. In the evaluation process, not only financial but also social and environmental aspects on operational, tactical and strategic levels should be taken into consideration: one should collect and interpret essential data, information and knowledge in compliance with required principles, criteria and use of suitable methods. Simple cash flow-based tools and discounted cash flow analysis are insufficient.

In the process of selecting methods and systems for comprehensive evaluation, one takes advantage of the current state of knowledge in business and management sciences and achievements concerning, in particular, evaluation methods of strategic, non-commercial, public, developmental and European projects. This scientific achievement and specifically experiences in evaluating the European project field are particularly useful.

Interesting multi-criteria evaluation solutions designed for multi-aspect and complex projects are recommended in various European Commission guidance documents and they are generally categorized in two independent perspectives: PCM/LFA and EVALSED (Fig. 2.5). The first involves the parallel use of the PCM methodology and the Logical Framework Approach (LFA), based on the Logical Framework Matrix (LFM) (Russo and Rindone 2009). The second perspective, evaluation of socio-economic development (EVALSED) is being developed at the request of the DG Regio—the Directorate General for Regional Policy. EVALSED involves online resources, intended for decision-makers dealing with the evaluation of projects, programs and socio-economic development policies. These resources include evaluation methods, techniques and tools, for example, beneficiary surveys, regression analysis and others (EVALSED 2013).

The PCM/LFA perspective provides comprehensive methodical support for the planning, execution, completion and final evaluation of various complex projects, for example, infrastructure projects concerning building national highways (Kim et al. 2008) and applying acquired experiences as well as best practices in the future. In this perspective, the relationship between an organizational strategic framework and its execution, as a result of projects, is ensured. The division into specific relatively small steps of the whole cycle facilitates decision-making processes associated

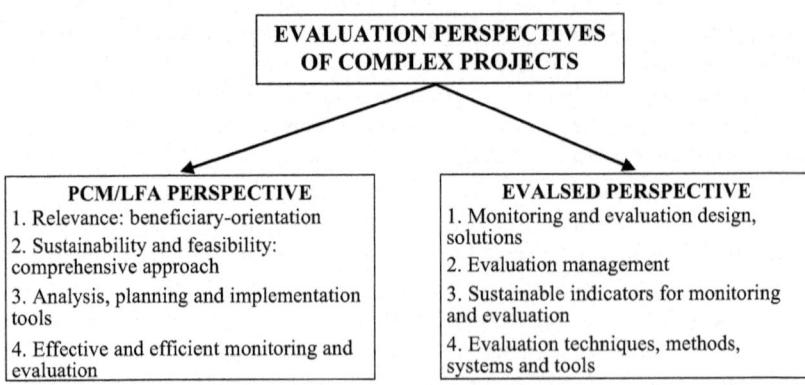

Fig. 2.5 Two independent perspectives of comprehensive project evaluation development

with the progressively implemented stages. Efficient and effective implementation of the project management function (planning, organizing, coordinating and controlling) is additionally supported by a set of tools for project design and management associated with the LFA approach.

The EVALSED perspective supports research focused on the evaluation process of relatively large projects and provides information which refers mainly to fragmentary methods useful at different stages of complex projects' evaluation processes. It was published earlier in the paper form in a multi-volume edition, known as the MEANS collection (Methods for Evaluating Action of a Structural Nature) (MEANS Collection 1999).

In many classical evaluation approaches and in the aforementioned modern perspectives (e.g. PCM/LFA and EVALSED), the Goal Oriented Project Planning (GOPP) conception plays a major role. The significant influence of this conception is also visible in recently built models using different levels of goals (operational objective, project purpose and global objective) and performed on three different levels: operational, tactical and strategic. For example, the Trocki model was built with the use of a holistic way of thinking, taking into consideration the two following perspectives (worlds): ideas (imaginations and expectations) and facts (consequences and project results) (Trocki 2012). The first perspective (ideas) concerns the stakeholder needs to be satisfied, the processes of project design, planned activities, planned outputs and project objectives, project inputs and costs. The second one (facts) refers to satisfied stakeholder needs, implemented activities, achieved outputs and project objectives.

Modeling processes of comprehensive evaluation systems may also be realized with the use of inspiration derived from interdisciplinary research results and some integrated approaches, which can include influences from business and management sciences, general systems theory (Bertalanffy L. von. 1973), general theory of effective and purposeful human action (praxeology), AI and knowledge engineering.

Building comprehensive systems is only one of the possible directions of research connected with evaluation models, methods and systems. In most cases, evaluation methods and systems are not comprehensive. Integration of quantitative and qualitative methods, along with application of AI methods in one system, provides the opportunity to build a comprehensive mixed systems approach for project evaluation. It is also confirmed by other research on plurality of methods in project evaluation (Woolcock 2009).

2.5   AI Systems for Evaluation

Processed socio-economic data are usually not precisely determined or are measured with an assumed margin of error. Empirical data, information and knowledge gained empirically, which is crucial in evaluation research, are often uncertain, blurred, fuzzy and difficult to present in numerical form. AI methods are an essential complement to the collection of evaluation methods applied in comprehensive evaluation systems because they may be used to solve decision problems under uncertainty conditions. AI usefulness is confirmed, in particular, when gathered knowledge is incomplete, and such methods and systems can be an important supplement in cases where classical approaches fail.

In general, AI methods can be divided into strong AI methods and weak AI methods. The first type of methods concerns modeling and creating artificial systems that think and behave like humans, and until recently research in this field has been carried out quite rarely and mostly reffered to the future. Currently, weak AI methods are used to solve problems within operations research as well as business and management sciences, and these can be useful for building single and integrated models for comprehensive project evaluation systems. These methods are based on mathematical models, which result from, among others, biological and mathematical inspirations.

AI methods, called soft computing methods, are different from conventional hard computing methods with closely defined functions and based on unchangeable algorithms. They are well suited for solving poorly structured problems specific to the evaluation of complex projects. Prior research results have confirmed the usefulness of AI methods for solving such problems (Grzeszczyk 2005).

AI methods are an intrinsic part of computer science, but the most interesting real-world applications and results are obtained by carrying out scientific research on the boundaries of different sciences, for example formal sciences (formal language disciplines such as mathematics, logic, statistics, systems theory, decision theory etc.), social sciences (economics, political science, business and management sciences, psychology, sociology, linguistics etc.), natural sciences (biology, chemistry, physics etc.) and interdisciplinary sciences.

AI methods allow the working out of models and implementation of learning systems which can be applied for discovering knowledge in data sets, knowledge management, generating decision rules and clearing up particular project situations and can be used for the generalization of empirical knowledge that is useful in processes of project evaluation.

Multifaceted and comprehensive models of evaluation improvement, based on AI systems, may rely on the use of the iterative approach in which there are separate sequences of iteratively repeated actions that allow realization of continuous and multi-aspect processes of improving comprehensive project evaluation (Grzeszczyk 2012). Such a dynamic system is based on a constantly updated rule-based knowledge base that can be developed, improved and served to record unstructured qualitative evaluation factors, referring to the knowledge resources of experts performing an evaluation (taking into consideration their experience, qualifications and attitudes).

Stages within these iterative models of project evaluation improvement are set chronologically in sequential form and are repeated many times in the feedback loop (Fig. 2.6). Each of the repeated sequences of the iterative model consists of four stages: objectives and evaluation principles determination, information and knowledge gathering, learning process

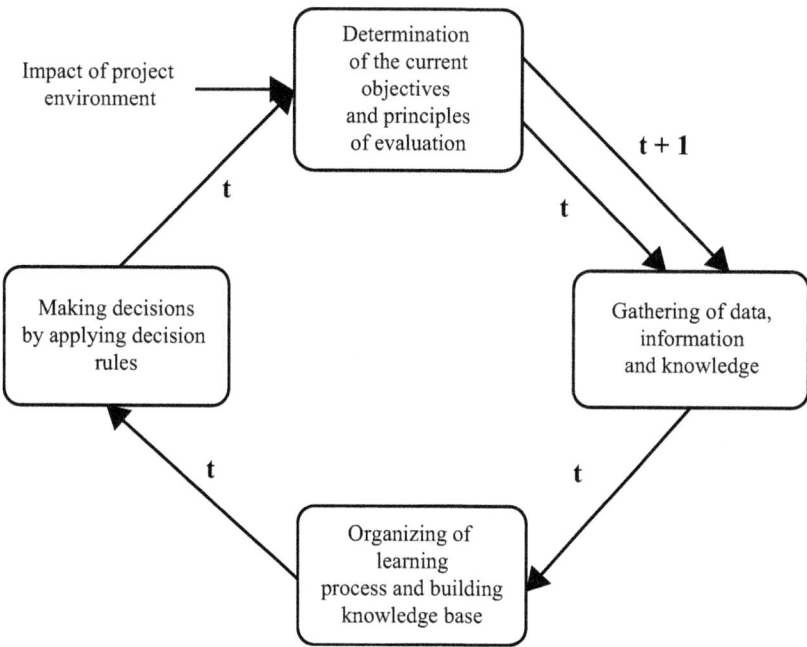

Fig. 2.6 Rule-based iterative model of project evaluation improvement. (Source: Based on Grzeszczyk (2012))

organization and project evaluation determination. Within the first one, the establishment of the main objectives and principles for a given iteration is done. In the second stage, the collection of information and knowledge about project evaluation is gathered. The third stage concerns evaluation of knowledge discovery and building rules that are meters of evaluation. In the last, fourth stage, a multi-criteria projects sorting process is created, with the use of decision rules (Grzeszczyk 2012).

AI systems can be applied successfully to detect hidden relationships between socio-economic data in sets of empirical learning objects concerning evaluated projects. Both classical solutions and AI based systems may be used in quantitative and qualitative project evaluation research.

2.6   Quantitative Versus Qualitative Methods

Typically, there is not just one method of project evaluation. Thus, there is need for using a number of quantitative and qualitative methods, whose application in evaluation research makes it possible to obtain useful information about the project and allows us to formulate its evaluation.

Among the many quantitative evaluation methods, we can distinguish the following: surveys, application of existing databases, statistical analysis and new quantitative methods based on AI. Essential complements to these quantitative methods are the following qualitative evaluation methods: non-statistical analysis, case study, observation, field investigation, issue mapping and logic models.

Quantitative and qualitative methods are fundamentally different from each other and are used to study different kind of problems. They are characterized by diverse philosophical roots and extensions and are used to fulfill a variety of research purposes.

Qualitative methods are mainly based on general descriptions of the evaluated reality, discovering hidden cause-effect relationships through extended systematic observation as well as on the knowledge and experience of experts. They are, therefore, subject to errors arising from their subjectivity. Qualitative research locates the observer in a particular situation, turns it into a sequence of representations, including interviews, photographs, conversations, recordings, field notes and notes to the self, which make the world visible (Given 2008). Qualitative analysis concerns studying how people construct meaning; it is essential to determine what is meaningful and to discover substantively meaningful themes and patterns (Patton 2015).

Quantitative methods are used for gathering data mainly in numerical form and are more objective and focused on a clear quantitative measurement. They are easier for practical applications, interpretations of numerical results and can provide accurate, quantitative confirmation of qualitative and overall results of the qualitative research.

Quantitative analysis refers to data, for example, in tables (research reports, spreadsheet files etc.), and subjected to various statistical analyses, whereas qualitative analysis involves the systematic comparison as well as interpretation of unstructured information sources, applying interviews, documentation and cross-referencing (Tavistock Institute 2003). The use of quantitative methods is based on the philosophical mainstream of positivism, while qualitative methods are associated with interpretivism and constructivism.

Qualitative methods are more flexible, characterized by good properties in studies of attitudes and human behavior (e.g. in project stakeholder analysis). These methods often focus on small stakeholder groups, are poorly structured and require significant expert experience with their application. Quantitative methods are better structured; it is easier to quickly understand the essence of their use and ways of data gathering. For quantitative research, many professional and precision instruments and tools for data collection have been developed.

The correctness of project evaluation results with the use of qualitative methods depends mainly on the experience and skills of researchers. They are based on observations, procedures for analysis of documents and existing sources, focus group interviews and so on. Data sources may be used individually or together.

Proper quantitative and qualitative methods enable the building of mixed (integrated) models which are universal tools of comprehensive evaluation of various projects. The model to be built ensures the execution of comprehensive evaluation and several quantitative and qualitative criteria. Such a model can be dynamic and capture non-linear interactions, and it is easy to change the objectives and principles of the evaluation process conducted. Proper use of these methods requires the gathering of information about them.

References

Aid Delivery Methods. (2014). *Project Cycle Management Guidelines* (Vol. 1). Brussels: European Commission.

Bayney, R. M., & Chakravarti, R. (2012). *Enterprise Project Portfolio Management: Building Competencies for R&D and IT Investment Success.* Plantation: J. Ross Publishing.

Bertalanffy, L. von (1973). *General System Theory: Foundations, Development, Applications.* New York: G. Braziller.

Chen, H. T. (2004). *Practical Program Evaluation: Assessing and Improving Planning. Implementation, and Effectiveness.* California: SAGE Publications Inc. Thousand Oaks California 91320.

EVALSED. (2013). *The Resource for the Evaluation of Socio-Economic Development.* http://ec.europa.eu/regional_policy/sources/docgener/evaluation/guide/guide_evalsed.pdf. Accessed Nov 2017.

Gasik, S. (2015 , March). Project Families and Their Application for Project Evaluation. *PM World Journal, 4*(3), 1–14.

Gill, J., Johnson, P., & Clark, M. (2010). *Research Methods for Managers.* California: SAGE Publications Inc. Thousand Oaks California 91320.

Given, L. M. (2008). *The SAGE Encyclopedia of Qualitative Research Methods.* California: SAGE Publications Inc. Thousand Oaks California 91320.

Gray, I., & Manson, S. (2011). *The Audit Process: Principles, Practice and Cases.* Hampshire, UK: South-Western Cengage Learning EMEA.

Green, J., & South, J. (2006). *Evaluation.* Berkshire, England: Open University Press. McGraw-Hill Education. McGraw-Hill House.

Grzeszczyk, T. A. (2005). A Rough Set Method for Knowledge Management in the Process of Structural Funds Projects Preparation. *Journal of Tung Fang Institute of Technology, 25,* 257–271.

Grzeszczyk, T. A. (2012). *Modeling Evaluation of European Projects.* Warsaw: Placet. (In Polish).

Grzeszczyk, T. A. (2013a). Developing a New Project Evaluation Systems Based on Knowledge. *Foundations of Management, 5*(2), 59–68.

Grzeszczyk, T. A. (2013b). *Towards the Model of Comprehensive Project Evaluation System.* Warsaw: Faculty of Management, Warsaw University of Technology.

Gudda, P. A. (2011). *Guide to Project Monitoring & Evaluation.* Bloomington: Author House. 1663 Liberty Drive.

https://en.oxforddictionaries.com/definition/comprehensive. Accessed Oct 2017.

Kerzner, H. (2004). *Advanced Project Management: Best Practices on Implementation.* Hoboken, New Jersey: John Wiley & Sons, Inc.

Kim, J., Yoo, I., & Tsunokawa, K. (2008). Evaluation of PMS in Korea Using PCM Method. In E. K. Zavadskas, A. Kaklauskas, & M. J. Skibniewski (Eds.), *Proceedings of the 25th International Symposium on Automation and Robotics in Construction.* Vilnius, Lithuania: International Association for Automation and Robotics in Construction, Vilnius Gediminas Technical University.

Krishnaswamy, K. N., Sivakumar, A. I., & Mathirajan, M. (2009). *Management Research Methodology: Integration of Methods and Techniques.* New Delhi: Prentice Hall.

Little, T. D. (Ed.). (2013). *The Oxford Handbook of Quantitative Methods. Volume 1: Foundations.* New York: Oxford University Press, Inc. 198 Madison Avenue.

Lopez-Acevedo, G., Krause, P., & Mackay, K. (Eds.). (2012). *Building Better Policies: The Nuts and Bolts of Monitoring and Evaluation Systems.* Washington: World Bank Publications. 1818 H Street NW.

MEANS Collection. (1999). *Evaluating Socio-Economic Programmes.* A Set of Six Volumes. European Commission. DG-Regio. Luxembourg: Office for Official Publications of the European Communities.

Patton, M. Q. (2015). *Qualitative Research & Evaluation Methods. Integrating Theory and Practice.* Thousand Oaks/London/New Delhi: SAGE Publications Inc.

PMBOK Guide. (2017). *A Guide to the Project Management Body of Knowledge* (6th ed.). Pennsylvania: Project Management Institute.

Project Audit Methodology. (2018). http://www.projektmanazer.cz/sites/default/files/dokumenty/00projectauditmethodology.pdf. Accessed Feb 2018.

Reynolds, M., & Holwell, S. (Eds.). (2010). *Systems Approaches to Managing Change: A Practical Guide.* Milton Keynes: The Open University in Association with Springer-Verlag London Limited.

Rossi, P. H., Lipsey, M. W., & Freeman, H. E. (2004). *Evaluation: A Systematic Approach.* California: SAGE Publications Inc. Thousand Oaks California 91320.

Russo, F., & Rindone, C. (2009). *Safety of Users in Road Evacuation: Modelling and DSS for LFA in the Planning Process* (Vol. 120). Sustainable Development and Planning. WIT Transactions on Ecology and the Environment.

Sanderson, J. M. (2012). Strategic Planning and Program Management: Implementing an Organizational Strategic Vision Through a Disciplined Program Management Approach. In G. Levin (Ed.), *Program Management: A Life Cycle Approach.* Boca Raton: CRC Press. Taylor & Francis Group. 6000 Broken Sound Parkway NW.

Schiavo-Campo, S., & Tommasi, D. (1999). *Managing Government Expenditure.* Manila: Asian Development Bank.

Scriven, M. (1991). *Evaluation Thesaurus.* London: Sage Publications Inc.

Tavistock Institute. (2003). *The Evaluation of Socio-Economic Development: The Guide.* London: Tavistock Institute in association with GHK, IRS.

The New Programming Period 2007–2013. (2006). *Indicative Guidelines on Evaluation Methods: Ex ante Evaluation.* European Commission. Directorate-General Regional Policy.

Trocki, M. (2012). Comprehensive Evaluation of Projects. Studia i Prace Kolegium Zarządzania i Finansów. Scientific Notebook 113. Warsaw: Warsaw School of Economics. (In Polish).

Wang, V. C. X. (2017). *Handbook of Research on Program Development and Assessment Methodologies in K-20 Education.* Hershey PA, USA: IGI Global.

Wholey, J. S., Hatry, H. P., & Newcomer, K. E. (2010). *Handbook of Practical Program Evaluation.* San Francisco: Jossey-Bass, John Wiley & Sons Imprint.

Woolcock, M. (2009). Toward a Plurality of Methods in Project Evaluation: A Contextualized Approach to Understanding Impact Trajectories and Efficacy. *Journal of Development Effectiveness, 1*(1), 1–14.

www.dictionary.com/browse/comprehensive. Accessed Oct 2017.

Xie, L., & Yang, Y. (2011). A Study on Management Risk Evaluation System of Large-Scale Complex Construction Projects. In D. D. Wu (Ed.), *Modeling Risk Management in Sustainable Construction*. Berlin-Heidelberg: Springer-Verlag.

CHAPTER 3

Quantitative Evaluation Methods

Abstract This chapter concentrates on quantitative evaluation methods—both classical and AI based. At the beginning, the author offers some advice on ways of choosing primary and secondary data to be used in quantitative evaluation. Errors and imperfections in data collection can ultimately distort the quantitative evaluation's final results. Then, the chapter considers surveys and statistical analysis that allow evaluators to draw meaningful conclusions from research in which quantitative data are systematically gathered. Generally, statistics can be regarded as a science discipline dealing with quantitative research methods for studying processes with mass data, by using descriptive and inferential procedures. Descriptive procedures are applied for direct study concerning large amounts of data, whereas inferential procedures are used for indirect research, testing hypotheses and drawing conclusions regarding whole larger populations based on sample data sets. Methods based on AI presented at the end of the chapter facilitate work on modeling mixed intelligent systems, as analyzed in Chap. 6.

Keywords Quantitative evaluation • Surveys • Statistical analysis • Neural networks for evaluation

© The Author(s) 2018   27
T. A. Grzeszczyk, *Mixed Intelligent Systems,*
https://doi.org/10.1007/978-3-319-91158-8_3

3.1   Primary and Secondary Data

Quantitative data (numerical data) can be relatively easily analyzed and verified, collected from many diverse sources (such as surveys and questionnaires, interviews, focus groups, progress tracking systems, project documentation etc.) in order to build primary (direct measurement), secondary (data transfer and indirect gathering) and mixed (combination, integrated) data collections. Figure 3.1 shows the basic methods of data gathering.

The key advantage of primary collected data is that they harmonize with the particular project, the assumed research problems, the research objectives and the research questions (Ghauri and Gronhaug 2005). Errors and imperfections in data collection can ultimately distort an evaluation's final results. To manage this situation, the research team gathers as much data, information and knowledge about the project being evaluated as possible, which increases the exactness of later analysis outcomes. Increasing the scope of study, however, involves increasing the costs of conducting this kind of research.

In view of this, primary data captured during the evaluation processes is usually very labor-intensive, time-consuming, expensive, tedious and error-prone. Thus, evaluators search for existing data resources, for

Fig. 3.1 Methods of data collection. (Source: Based on MEANS Collection (1999))

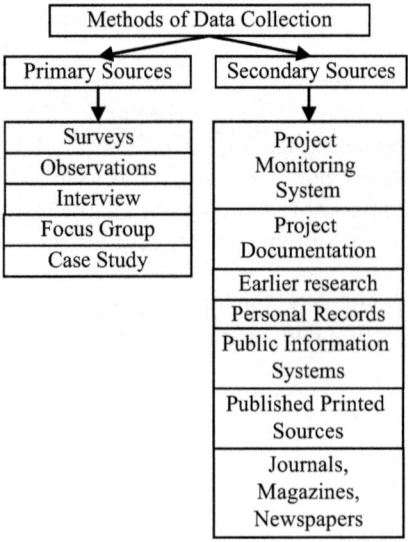

example from the documentation of previously performed projects and their evaluation reports, monitoring systems, public databases and statistics systems, and so on.

Useful data sources may have an internal character (directly related to the evaluated project or other projects, programs and portfolios undertaken by the organization) or can come from external resources, such as governments and administrative data systems, public information systems (in the private sector and in the public sector), national and international trade association websites, archived academic surveys, commercial services, local, national or international statistical institutions and other Internet sources.

Reliable and useful for carrying out evaluation processes, secondary data (in the indicators form) can come from project monitoring systems. Monitoring indicators (measurable, realistic criteria) reflect project progress toward obtaining project outcomes. In addition to these indicators, useful secondary data may result from current research, for example connected with other similar projects in an organization.

When monitoring systems do not meet the evaluators' expectations, are not sufficient for evaluation processes, state sources of incorrect, inconsistent and incomplete data, have limited functionality, may contain only selected information (e.g. financial) and there are no other results of already completed studies in the organization, some additional research should be carried out to supplement the missing data. In such cases integrated data collections become useful.

3.2   SURVEYS

Survey research is based on the technique of sampling (selected population subgroups answering predefined questions) and questionnaire tools in paper or electronic form, consisting of thematically structured series of questions.

The sampling technique is based on generalizing research results concerning a part (the sample) of a larger population; and the proper selection and application of the sampling procedure is crucial to ensuring proper representation of the target population through this sample. Questionnaires are used as a communication medium between the researcher and the interviewers from whom the desired information is received (Brace 2008).

The main difference between survey and interview research methods lies in the fact that survey questionnaires are usually self-completed without the participation of researchers (structured interview without invigilators), and interviews are conducted face-to-face by trained interviewers. Survey research is much simpler, cheaper and can be used for larger interviewing groups, compared to the interview method which is time-consuming and requires significant financial outlays.

The fundamental problem in survey research preparation is proper and appropriate survey (closed- and open-ended) question preparation, which should be clear to project stakeholders and asked in the correct order (sensitive and tricky questions at the end of the research). Closed-ended questions are easy for quantitative counting and statistical analysis of particular types of pre-determined responses which cannot be ambiguous and overlapping. In the case of open-ended questions, survey respondents complete a questionnaire using their own words and it is assumed that they have some knowledge on specific topics.

Survey questions may be delivered to research participants through e-mail and questionnaire web pages (low-cost methods, and unfortunately a low response rate), by mobile (much higher cost and response rates), Skype (sometimes connection and sound problems occur) or face-to-face (the most expensive and the most accurate method). Face-to-face methods (individual stakeholder interviews) are not always possible or accepted by the project stakeholders.

Evaluators usually face considerable difficulties in obtaining a sufficiently high response rate and encourage stakeholders to fill out questionnaires. Answers inscribed in questionnaires are frequently less objective, especially for open-ended questions. Survey participants sometimes have a tendency toward overly negative or too positive attitudes, affecting the subjectivity of the answers provided.

3.3   STATISTICAL ANALYSIS

Statistical analysis allows evaluators to draw meaningful conclusions from their research: quantitative data are systematically gathered through, for example, observation, surveys, simulation, experimentation and so on. Such analysis, allowing the testing of small samples of a larger population, enables the receipt of worthwhile and precise results, ensuring their generalizability and plays a fundamental role in analyzing data in evaluation processes.

Applying sophisticated statistical procedures is quite intensive and requires sophisticated knowledge about statistics. This should not lead to the abandonment of advanced methods and statistical tools. Application simplicity cannot be the primary criterion for the choice of such instruments, but it should be taken into consideration when making evaluation more meaningful, with results that are more comprehensible for stakeholders (Russ-Eft and Preskill 2009).

Generally, statistics can be regarded as a science discipline dealing with quantitative research methods for studying processes with mass data, by using descriptive and inferential procedures. Descriptive statistics concern methods of summarizing and reducing data, and making their key features more transparent in a human sense, for example, due to calculating simple means, variances or plotting histograms (Everitt and Skrondal 2010).

Descriptive statistics is suitable and leads to useful results for the study of entire populations for relatively small projects involving a limited number of stakeholders. This kind of statistics can be used to present associations linking certain variables to others and to create synthetic summaries about the data sets.

For statistical analyses carried out for the evaluation of larger projects, programs and portfolios, it is impossible to investigate the entire stakeholders' population and thus quantitative data are gathered from only a population sample, representing the whole target population. Descriptive statistics procedures are then useful in order to describe the features of this sample data. Drawing objective conclusions concerning the quantitative data relating to the entire population, based on sample data analysis, is possible with the use of inferential statistical procedures.

In summary, descriptive procedures are applied for direct study concerning large amounts of data, whereas inferential procedures are used for indirect research, testing hypotheses and drawing conclusions regarding whole larger populations based on sample data sets.

Figure 3.2 shows the way of choosing more common statistical research procedures related to descriptive and inferential statistics.

Among statistical modeling methods based on inferential procedures, an important role is played by regression analysis applied to a study and approximation of the relationships between variables. Regression functions are used to explain relationships between one variable (the dependent, explained, response) and other variables (independent, predictor, explanatory) analytically. In this type of statistical modeling, fundamental elements of built models are regressive equations including independent variables and dependent variables, all of which usually have a quantitative character.

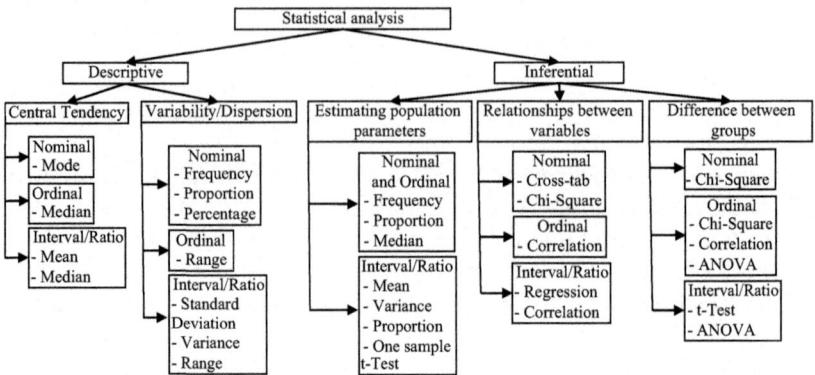

Fig. 3.2 Choosing appropriate statistical research procedures. (Source: Based on Ukaga and Maser (2003))

Econometric regression models are useful solutions concerning the determination of formal descriptions of relationships occurring in the environments of evaluated projects. Such models can be applied, for instance, to investigate causal relationships between dependent and independent variables, as well as to analyze the cause-effect relationships in project evaluation processes. The cause has the form of certain project implementations, while results are set as outcomes and impacts which possibly occur as effects of this implementation.

Causal relationships can be both deductive and inductive. Deductive models enable the checking of hypotheses (usually concerning explanations of cause-and-effect relationships occurring between implemented projects and their positive as well as negative effects), based on the collected empirical data.

An effective method for deductive testing of causal relationships between factors connected with evaluated projects can be, for example, based on regression analysis. Achieving certain effects in the case of inductive models means determining real causes that result from the fact of project realization or may be totally independent of it. Examples of regression model applications in the determination of the percentage of positive results achieved by evaluated projects implementation are shown in the following publications: (MEANS Collection 1999; Grzeszczyk 2010).

Another statistical method, shift-share analysis (comparative static model), often applied in regional studies and local economic development planning, is based on a mathematical model set, the use of which leads to the identification of time scale changes taking place as a result of public intervention and project implementation, whose outcomes are usually presented in the visual form of graphs and diagrams. This analysis can be used as an overall evaluation method, applied, for example, in the case of development and public projects implemented to solve problems connected with sustainable development.

Problems from the closest surroundings of evaluated projects are observed and investigated through the prism of further surroundings. Positive changes in project evaluation indicators referring to nearer local surroundings that differ significantly from the tendency in broader (regional and national) contexts might suggest a positive impact of the implemented project. Changes analyzed are broken down into the three following elements regarding project or program effects: local share, industry mix and national share (Blakely and Leigh 2010).

Shift-share analysis, among other analytical methods, uses trend extrapolation techniques (Sinha and Labi 2007) and allows the approximate identification of the sources of regional and local changes, as well as to which degree an implemented project has a beneficial impact on its surroundings. The outcomes and impact of evaluated projects are quantitatively evaluated by moving trends from further surroundings to the level of closer surroundings that a particular project is directly connected with.

Figure 3.3 shows an example of the application of a shift-share analysis carried out to evaluate the impact of a large project or program on the regional employment level. The analysis is based on a quantitative impact estimation, by transferring national trends to the regional level to which the evaluated project or program is related. The likely effects of the project may result from the difference between the current employment level in the region (54,000) and the hypothetical level of employment (51,000) which occurs in the case of applying the national trend when the employment level is determined.

The hypothetical example presented concerns one of many aspects of projects and programs supporting the fight against unemployment. On the basis of such analysis, it is difficult to evaluate projects regarding unemployment objectively, because an increase in the employment level can have many underlying reasons and, for example, might involve a change in the local population.

Statistical methods such as shift-share are not usually used as the only methods in the process of multi-aspect evaluation. The results of a

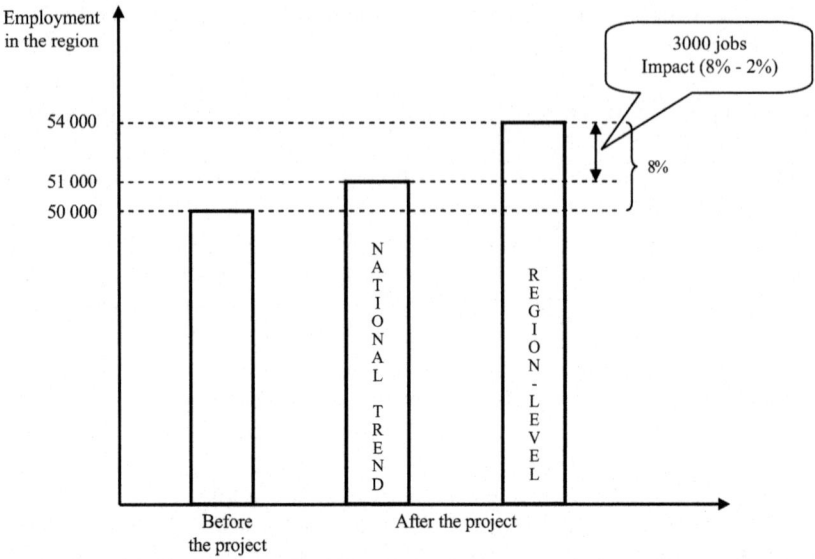

Fig. 3.3 Shift-share analysis of regional employment. (Source: Based on MEANS Collection (1999))

shift-share analysis show some tendencies and directions of changes, as well as potentially acting as an introduction to further study and advanced statistical analyses, confirming preliminary approximate results established from the analysis. Another useful solution is to integrate the results with qualitative evaluation methods related to expert surveys (Kovaleva and Baleevskih 2014).

Different kinds of statistical analyses (e.g. applied regression models) and various econometric models involve the use of high-tech statistical platforms which are difficult to apply. Using statistical procedures requires sophisticated knowledge from evaluators, of not only of statistical techniques and methods but also of the proper handling of statistical software tools.

Currently, open source analytics/data science tools such as Python and R-language, which are relatively difficult to learn, are the most popular within the Data Science market (according to the 2017 KDnuggets Poll results) (www.kdnuggets.com 2017). The Gartner 2017 Magic Quadrant for Data Science Platforms, based on completeness of vision and ability to execute, which concerns only commercial vendors, considered as leaders in this field IBM, SAS, RapidMiner and KNIME (www.kdnuggets.com 2017).

At the present time, Python and R-software have higher popularity than, for example, RapidMiner or SAS, probably because of free of charge access to these and their popularity among university students. RapidMiner is user-friendly and very intuitive in advanced applications. The R-software has excellent possibilities for statistical computing, but it is more difficult for many applications, especially for beginners.

In quantitative data analysis using such software, in addition to the classical statistical methods, AI models are also used. More information on this subject can be found in the next section, concerning new quantitative methods for evaluation based on artificial intelligence.

3.4   QUANTITATIVE EVALUATION BASED ON AI

The last point of this chapter includes methodological considerations about new quantitative methods for evaluation based on AI. A synthesis of scientific achievements in this field as well as opportunities for designing and implementing evaluation systems based on AI methods is outlined.

AI methods are characterized by versatility and the multi-aspect capabilities of various applications, and there are many methods with different possibilities that are potentially available for quantitative evaluation. In order to obtain satisfactory results, it is necessary to make an appropriate selection of methods suitable for solving specific research problems.

It can be assumed that quantitative AI methods may have a deductive character, and that their purpose is to deduce in accordance with top-down logical deduction which is based on a reasoning process: to reach certain specific conclusions drawn from some general statements. These methods are used to analyze the previously collected quantitative data in order to reach conclusions relating to the projects evaluated. The stages of collecting quantitative data and conducting an analysis are clearly separated.

Accepting assumptions about the purely quantitative or qualitative nature of certain AI methods is a kind of simplification. In practice, selected AI methods can be used in both types of reasoning processes: deductive (called top-down logic) and inductive (bottom-up logic— explained further on in the chapter devoted to qualitative methods).

AI methods are rather qualitative in nature and are less useful for obtaining results in numerical form, which are defined strictly and precisely. AI models, used in numerical calculations, are frequently difficult to design and describe precisely, and their results often do not have a formal character in which one can have full confidence. One can trust or reject the results obtained by using AI methods, as they are similar to the results given by experts who estimate predicted quantitative values without providing a justification. Some of the results are often difficult to fully explain. For example, in the case of both human forecasts and predictions and those based on artificial intelligence, the best assessment of uncertain forecasts is ex-post evaluations (comparison of predicted values with real ones).

AI methods are associated by many researchers with Artificial Neural Networks (ANNs) and sometimes Interdisciplinary Connectionist Systems (ICS) which are based on selected approaches chosen for specific applications and based on biologically inspired, non-symbolic knowledge representation (Gaweda et al. 2018). ANNs are modeled on biological systems, working in a parallel way to neural networks (consisting of many simple nerve cells) from which human and animal brains are built, but they constitute only much simplified mathematical models.

When building an ICS, for example, one can draw inspiration from such fields as cognitive science, AI, knowledge engineering, neuroscience, philosophy of mind and psychology, but in practice, ICS usually takes the ANN form. Both solutions, the more general ICS and the special case of ANN, can play a significant part in decision-making processes concerning evaluation.

An ANN is created by nodes (artificial neurons) connected with each other by synapses with weights that serve for transmitting signals, which are usually real numbers. Networks with neurons, usually organized in layers, are characterized by initial non-symbolic knowledge resulting from this kind of network, a structure of connections between neurons and values of the weights of synapses. The network learning process lies mainly in adjustment of the values of weights of the connections between neurons.

A type of network, a structure of connections between neurons and the initial values of synapse weights is the most often selected experimentally, because precise mathematical relations which can be used for designing networks are unknown. The correct design of an ANN is not an easy task, although it might seem so. Most of all, experiences, intuition and practical skills are important for this type of analysis.

Building and improving project evaluation models based on ANN systems results from the fact that new, unsymbolic knowledge resulting from learning processes and the accumulation of experience is stored in networks. The basic process associated with building and improving project evaluation models based on ANN systems is recording in networks new, non-symbolic knowledge resulting from learning processes and accumulation of experience. Learning processes can take place in the following three ways: unsupervised learning (without teacher), supervised learning (with teacher, desired classification or learning purposes) and hybrid learning.

In the case of systems based on unsupervised learning, in input data sets, the discovery of potentially useful patterns (dependencies, groups—clusters) is made and there is no known classification (correct answers to the learning system). The supervised learning system learns from a training set with Input/Output (I/O) pairs. In this case, training data sets including learning examples are used and the network is informed about classifying objects (e.g. evaluated projects) to certain decision classes related to various evaluations. Hybrid learning systems learn from a relatively small number of I/O pairs and most learning cases have unknown classifications.

ANNs typically require a long-term learning process, frequently realized with the use of learning example sets, which include input information and corresponding output information (a resultant categorization or classification is included and connected with relevant observations). Unsupervised ANN learning is less frequently used and assumes no use of supervisory I / O training data sets containing examples with some determined categorization or classification.

An important and useful feature of ANNs is their capability for knowledge generalization, which means the ability to generalize experiences gained in the process of network learning. Thanks to this feature, ANN outputs can receive the right signals, even for input information which was not in the learning set before.

A significant advantage of ANN which can be applied in project evaluation processes is the relative simplicity of models created through their use and the wide range of applications. Although ANNs learn over a long time, they quickly work at the stage of using the acquired knowledge to solve desired problems connected with project evaluation.

Neural networks also have important disadvantages, and in many cases, they produce weak results. Generally, in research processes using ANN there are often difficulties in evaluating the obtained results. These difficulties are associated with non-symbolic knowledge representation (unreadable to humans) obtained as a result of learning process realization. This form of knowledge representation is the consequence of the distributed and parallel processing of information by neurons and the creation of knowledge through modification of connection weights occurring between a considerable number of neurons.

A typical procedure for building a neural model is as follows:

- empirical data preparation,
- selection of one of the available network types,
- determination of the model's architecture,
- performing of the learning, validation and network testing processes,
- neural model assessment,
- completing the construction of the model or starting construction of the next one,
- application of the neural model for regression analysis.

Certain input signals are delivered through ANN inputs and processed by the network, causing the creation of output signals. In many cases ANN methods are treated as 'black-box methods' and few researchers are interested in the contents of this box. ANNs have a huge range of applications, and are relatively easy to use, but regardless of progress in development of this type of non-symbolic knowledge representation systems, the parts of symbolic structures used to represent background/domain knowledge have a basic meaning in intelligent systems implementation (Kriegel and Aylett 2008). More details on modeling different economic problems with the use of ANN can be found in the extensive literature from this field (Galushkin 2007).

Apart from ANN, biological inspirations relate to genetic algorithms and evolutionary algorithms which are the larger class of such methods used in operations research within business and management sciences. Their activity is based on mechanisms observed in nature: growth, functioning, interactions, the fight for survival of individuals and populations, as well as key bio-inspired operations (mutation, selection and crossover). This set of population of individuals usually determines acceptable solutions for searching for and optimizing of problems studied.

Among others, genetic algorithms, genetic programming, evolution programming, evolution strategies and so on are included in concepts connected with evolutionary algorithms, as described in many publications (Rothlauf 2006; Yang et al. 2007).

Genetic algorithms are a metaheuristic inspiration and have some quantitative applications, but to a large extent this is qualitative. In practice, some AI methods have an inductive character: their goal is reasoning according to bottom-up logic (from specific empirical observations and measures to broader generalizations) and their application in qualitative analyses is indicated. On the other hand, it is possible to reverse them and implement activities that are characteristic for the deductive drawing of conclusions and quantitative analyses.

Considerations presented in the next chapter concern the complementary role of qualitative methods in building a model of mixed intelligent systems for project evaluation. A combined application of many different data analysis methods supports the comprehensive project evaluation process and allows the receiving of an integrated, quantitative and qualitative approach to knowledge.

References

Blakely, E. J., & Leigh, N. G. (2010). *Planning Local Economic Development: Theory and Practice*. California: SAGE Publications Inc. Thousand Oaks California 91320.

Brace, I. (2008). *Questionnaire Design: How to Plan, Structure and Write Survey Material for Effective Market Research*. London: Kogan Page.

Everitt, B. S., & Skrondal, A. (2010). *The Cambridge Dictionary of Statistics*. New York: Cambridge University Press.

Galushkin, A. I. (2007). *Neural Networks Theory*. Berlin-Heidelberg: Springer.

Gaweda, A. E., Kacprzyk, J., Rutkowski, L., & Yen, G. G. (Eds.). (2018). *Advances in Data Analysis with Computational Intelligence Methods: Dedicated to Professor Jacek Zurada*. 6330 Cham, Switzerland: Springer International Publishing AG.

Ghauri, P., & Gronhaug, K. (2005). *Research Methods in Business Studies: A Practical Guide*. London: Prentice Hall.

Grzeszczyk, T. A. (2010). Neural Networks Usage in the Evaluation of European Union Cofinanced Projects. *Foundations of Management, 2*(1), 7–20.

https://www.kdnuggets.com/2017/02/gartner-2017-mq-data-science-platforms-gainers-losers.html. Accessed Dec 2017.

https://www.kdnuggets.com/2017/05/poll-analytics-data-science-machine-learning-software-leaders.html. Accessed Dec 2017.

Kovaleva, T. Y., & Baleevskih, V. G. (2014). Identification of the Educational Clusters in the Regional Economy: Theory, Methodology and Research Results (In Example of Perm Krai). *International Journal of Econometrics and Financial Management, 2*(4), 153–162.

Kriegel, M., & Aylett, R. (2008). Emergent Narrative as a Novel Framework for Massively Collaborative. In H. Prendinger, M. Ishizuka, & J. Lester (Eds.), *Intelligent Virtual Agents: 8th International Conference. IVA 2008. Tokyo. Japan. September 1–3. Proceedings.* Lecture Notes in Computer Science/ Lecture Notes in Artificial Intelligence. Berlin-Heidelberg: Springer-Verlag.

MEANS Collection. (1999). *Evaluating Socioeconomic Programmes. Principal Evaluation Techniques and Tools* (Vol. 3). Luxembourg: European Commission Structural Funds.

Rothlauf, F. (2006). *Representations for Genetic and Evolutionary Algorithms.* Berlin-Heidelberg: Springer-Verlag.

Russ-Eft, D., & Preskill, H. (2009). *Evaluation in Organizations: A Systematic Approach to Enhancing Learning, Performance and Change.* New York: Basic Books.

Sinha, K. C., & Labi, S. (2007). *Transportation Decision Making: Principles of Project Evaluation and Programming.* Hoboken, New Jersey: John Wiley & Sons, Inc.

Ukaga, O., & Maser, C. (2003). *Evaluating Sustainable Development: Giving People a Voice in Their Destiny.* Sterling, Virginia: Stylus Publishing.

Yang, S., Ong, Y., & Jin, Y. (Eds.). (2007). *Evolutionary Computation in Dynamic and Uncertain Environments. Studies in Computational Intelligence* (Vol. 51). Berlin-Heidelberg: Springer.

CHAPTER 4

Qualitative Evaluation Methods

Abstract The qualitative evaluation methods presented in this chapter play a complementary role to the quantitative methods referred to in the previous chapter of this book. The author shows wider aspects regarding qualitative research, in addition to detailed remarks concerning fieldwork observation. In the latter part the chapter deals with logic models supporting two key evaluator challenges: measuring expected and achieved project outcomes and attributing these outcomes to specific project activities, based on the application of theory-based approaches. It is essential in the case of development, public and European projects, nevertheless, that the author should encourage these models to be introduced within the wider scope of different projects, including business-related situations. The end of the chapter focuses on the applications of new qualitative intelligent systems. Such systems should not only support the analysis of available qualitative data, but should also be characterized by machine intelligence, as a result of discovering knowledge from data that can be observed subjectively, suggesting specific decision rules, adapting to a particular project situation and the specific needs of researchers and evaluators.

Keywords Qualitative evaluation research • Fieldwork observation • Logic models • Qualitative intelligent systems

© The Author(s) 2018
T. A. Grzeszczyk, *Mixed Intelligent Systems,*
https://doi.org/10.1007/978-3-319-91158-8_4

4.1   QUALITATIVE RESEARCH

Inductive reasoning related to qualitative research is based on conducting empirical research and specific observations, aiming to obtain vast sets of data records, information and empirical knowledge about a particular project reality to be evaluated. Coding, simplifying, organizing, categorizing, discovering patterns and regularities, drawing conclusions, determining their properties as a result of, for example, a graphical and a matrix/table view of data, are carried out. Such activities enable efficient data exploration and, as a consequence, the obtaining of some general conclusions about the evaluated project reality.

In contrast to quantitative analyses (where data are first collected and then analyzed) in the case of qualitative research it is difficult to separate the data collection and analysis processes so clearly. In a sense, the processes of collecting and analyzing data take place in a parallel way, since qualitative research is implemented as a continuous process consisting of iteratively repeated sequences of actions. As a result of conducting this type of research with the use of qualitative methods, general models may be created, and some potentially useful patterns, information, knowledge and themes, for example, from interview texts with project stakeholders are also discovered.

Quantitative and statistical methods are a well-defined, well-studied area of research and are described in the literature in detail (Martin and Bridgmon 2012). Their importance in the process of comprehensive project evaluation is usually limited to certain aspects of operational levels, while tactical and strategic levels do not play a significant role.

The need to apply qualitative research emerges for the analysis of problems that are not easily quantifiable, unstable, often changing in a turbulent environment, or requiring observation in natural settings, such as, encounters, practices, episodes, groups, organizations, roles, relationships, social worlds and subcultures or lifestyles (Babbie 2008). Qualitative research often requires long-term and close contact between evaluators and project stakeholders (during collection and ongoing data analysis), as opposed to quantitative research which assumes only short-term contact when collecting data.

Qualitative research works well in the case of holistic analyses of strategic fundamental issues requiring a full and wide analysis of the long-term effects of projects and programs and the presentation of results in non-numerical forms, for example, in-depth written descriptions reflecting expert opinions on evaluated phenomena. The results of such research processes are not very formalized descriptions of observations, paper records or records in an electronic version concerning expert statements and interviews with project stakeholders.

Patton emphasizes, in relation to evaluation processes, the importance of the following types of qualitative data (Patton 2002):

- resulting from the proper conducting of interviews (containing not only their exact content, but also the characterized research context),
- collected as a result of using various methods of observation, including reliable characteristics of fieldwork descriptions of behaviors, project environment, interpersonal interactions and others,
- recorded in both paper and electronic versions (with clearly identified contexts for the collection of such data).

Qualitative data can also be collected from records of unstructured conversations with project stakeholders, and from graphs, photographs, journals, old evaluation reports, archival documents and so on.

From the point of view of mixed research methods and systems, research related to qualitative data can be an important complement to quantitative analyses. This is especially important in the case of comprehensive studies, for which many aspects are numerically immeasurable. Thanks to qualitative research, the results of quantitative research (conducted at operational and tactical levels) can be developed and made useful also on the strategic level. It is also possible to reverse the situation when the research is performed in accordance with qualitative research first and the quantitative research carried out later allows obtaining precise numerical results, making it possible to formulate more objective conclusions included in the final evaluation report. Application of computer systems and multimedia systems, such as audio monitoring, video recording and computer monitoring can support appropriate collection of qualitative data (Stawarski and Phillips 2008).

The advantages of qualitative research include the significance of the results obtained for the entire evaluation process (also conducted with the use of quantitative methods), flexibility, depth of understanding and usually low implementation costs, but their drawbacks are lower reliability and limited suitability for testing large populations (and obtaining descriptions of these) (Babbie 2008).

In qualitative research, there is only an approximate outline of the plan for the next stages of the research process. In contrast to quantitative research methods that require a precise and unambiguously determined procedure (unchanged for the various problems analyzed), qualitative research methods allow flexibility of approach and the introduction of changes in research procedures during research, for example, as a result of information obtained during implementation. Qualitative research is therefore non-deterministic, close to soft systems methodology and supports the analysis of complex problems in conditions of uncertainty and evaluated project knowledge imperfections.

Examples of qualitative research stages might be as follows (Russ-Eft and Preskill 2009):

1. adoption of research assumptions,
2. checking the suitability of data and their preparation for further analysis (sometimes it is necessary to integrate data from various sources, collected using different methods),
3. analysis of prepared data, taking into account compliance with the adopted research assumptions and evaluation objectives, usefulness of the results obtained, evaluation standards and requirements related to the subsequent preparation of the project evaluation final report,
4. specifying categories and allocating different data to individual categories,
5. examining data in individual categories, identifying similarities, differences and dependencies between categories,
6. presentation of clear graphical results: tables, causal diagrams, graphs, matrices and flow charts,
7. analysis of graphical results and formulation of final conclusions.

It is essential for comprehensive evaluation to use qualitative methods such as non-statistical analysis, observation methods, field investigation (ethnographic observation), methods based on logic models, participative methods (stakeholder-based consultation, Metaplan, concept or issue mapping) and case studies.

In addition to the typical qualitative methods, which will be presented in the next sections, it is possible to distinguish methods that were originally associated with quantitative research, but their application in qualitative research is currently being developed. Such methods are based, for example, on Geographic Information Systems (GIS) that gather, organize, code and present in graphical form geographic information in a way that allows their summarization, categorization, discovery of the essential characteristics and interpretation in terms of evaluation and support in subsequent qualitative analyses.

GIS process graphic data on various aspects of evaluated projects and enable the illustration of, for example, the impact of project implementation on the natural environment, social phenomena and so on. This impact can be evaluated by comparing maps and charts relating to different periods: before implementation, during implementation and after implementation of the project. Detecting differences between individual images, it is possible, for example, to make mid-term and ex-post evaluations. While carrying out ex-ante evaluation, computer simulations can be performed, creating images of the desired future situation and comparing them with digital maps showing the current, less favorable conditions. The digital maps compared with each other are created as a result of integration of several layers appearing in the form of maps presenting various details concerning the geographical environment of the analyzed projects.

When building multi-layered maps, aerial and satellite images of areas covered by the project can be used, and the images created on this basis can be three-dimensional. GIS are universal and support the process of integration of analysis methods as they enable adding to the graphical geographical information the results of analyses performed using other quantitative and qualitative methods. Such systems constitute software for geographic presentation and analysis, but they may also have the functionality of evaluation decision support systems justified by the results of digital map analysis and other geocoded information used in project evaluation processes.

For example, they can be GIS/DSS (Decision Support Systems), GIS/EXP (Expert Systems), GIS/CAD (Computer Aided Design), GIS/DOC (Document Processing), GIS/FM (Facility Management), GIS/MODEL (Spatial Modeling), GIS/VISION (Animation Systems), GIS/IMAGE (Earth Image Processing) and GIS/LBS (Location Based Services). LBS make it possible to deliver spatial data to the GIS using mobile and field units. Assistive technologies include Global Positioning Systems (GPS), providing integration of data with their location and Mobile GIS, and facilitating ongoing data updates in the field using laptop computers, tablets and mobile phones.

GIS enable the easy input of data into the system—from stationary terminals and from portable computers belonging to mobile evaluators (e.g. those conducting fieldwork observations). They integrate into a common image: objects appearing on different layers of the digital map with collected data about the project. They provide the ability to store multimedia content related to the geographical environment of the project. They have many functions of spatial analysis, processing, forecasting and simulations carried out on the basis of information from the data collection phase. They have simple reporting mechanisms in the form of text and tabular printouts of statistical analysis results. They also have the option of presenting multimedia visualizations of digital maps, shown in different perspectives, depending on the layer that is the subject of the evaluator's interest.

Individual layers that make up a digital map can be printed together or individually. Depending on the needs of the evaluator, on the printout (or visualization on the monitor screen) the descriptions of, for example, the attributes of objects appearing on the map or the markers provided by the evaluator, may be visible or hidden. They have facilities of decision support systems in the form of modeling and simulation tools, facilitating the forecasting of the effects of the project (ex-ante evaluation) and spatial presentation after the completion of the project (ex-post evaluation). They facilitate conducting cause-effect analysis, justifying one rather than another evaluation of the project. They suggest the possibility of improving the unfavorable situation (bad project), providing various possible solutions to solve problems. They enable incremental data entry; for example tracking the progress of project implementation and analyzing geostatistical data entered in the next stages of task implementation. They facilitate simultaneous work by many users within the system and are characterized by good scalability, that is, with the development of the scope of the project they are relatively easy to expand; it is not difficult to use them (after simple modifications) to analyses data related to the evaluation of projects of varying complexity.

GIS are well suited for the evaluation of projects related to the development of ICT infrastructure and investment projects related to the implementation of, for example, infrastructure serving the supply of various types of utilities: water, sewage, gas, electricity and so on. Spatial visualizations of network elements (planned and existing in reality) allow for estimation of the level of investment implementation, with the division of networks into parts: planned for execution, already completed (but, e.g., unserviceable, unsettled) and existing and operating in accordance with project assumptions.

In addition to applications related to infrastructural projects, they can also be useful in the evaluation of projects combating unemployment (visualization of clusters of the unemployed), environmental protection (spatial presentation of threats), training (location of training centers in the field), advisory (location of advisory points for SMEs and microenterprises), revitalization of rural areas (location of facilities requiring modernization or removal) and planning of various types of investments in the field.

A significant difficulty associated with the development of GIS applications in project evaluation is the appropriate adaptation of digital maps to various spatial data related to evaluated projects and the ongoing updating of data from, for example, the monitoring system, fieldwork observations and stakeholder interviews. In principle, GIS should use geostatistical databases that are constantly edited by the evaluators, but data from the database edited by different people may be inconsistent after some time and cause significant errors and discrepancies. This mainly applies to qualitative data, which may be different for various contexts of their collection.

The level of qualifications, attitudes and psychophysical parameters are different for individual people from the evaluation team. To maintain the quality of the data (consistent and non-discrepant) stored in the integrated database, one of the evaluators should be appointed to become the administrator of the GIS and the central geostatistical database. It is his/her responsibility to update data related to the project being evaluated and its general geographical environment. It is necessary to adopt a uniform standard of interpretation of qualitative data entered into the GIS database and their later legible presentation (before and after the analysis).

4.2   Fieldwork Observation

Fieldwork (field investigation, field research, ethnographic observation)— one of the key qualitative research methods—is referred to, among other terms, as ethnographic research, because it was initiated by ethnographers who conducted observations of people appearing within their actual spatial systems (houses, streets, green areas, etc.) The great advantage of such research results from the realism of the activities of the surveyed people, whose behavior results from socio-cultural conditions. People in their natural environment behave naturally and are interesting objects that may be subject to observation in all their complexity. A large collection of relatively well-known methods is associated with fieldwork: observation, interviews, collective discussions, self-analysis, document analyses and others.

Field investigation means going to the 'field' where the evaluated project is being implemented. Observations, interviews and other research influence those who implement the project, as well as related stakeholders—in some ways they feel the effects of this implementation in a positive or negative way. Fieldwork involves going to the project site, observing the surroundings and conducting conversations (interviews) with people who are often accidentally encountered.

Fieldwork does not impose strict methodological and organizational limitations, which sometimes leads to difficulties related to the search for ways to conduct the research properly, and in particular the subsequent interpretation of the results. The implementation of this kind of research depends to a large extent on the characteristics of the person who performs it. Fieldwork evaluators should be able to interact easily with people and conduct with them non-targeted interviews in the form of loose conversations. They should have the ability to conduct systematic observations, be able to carry out the selection of relevant and unimportant information on an ongoing basis, and should skillfully record valuable data, using their ability to collect data objectively, that is, the ability to separate one's own opinions from judgments presented by the persons being examined.

Fieldwork makes it possible to notice determinants and complexity of the investigated phenomena that cannot be captured by other methods, for example, it is possible to study more closely motivations of the surveyed stakeholders that might not be correctly evaluated using surveys. On the basis of this type of research, it is often relatively easy to draw general conclusions and estimate the development trends of a given community through the simultaneous use of many research techniques, such as, interviews, surveys, document analysis and others. Analyses made with the use of qualitative data (e.g. obtained from observation), may be additionally supported by the analysis of quantitative data collected, for example, as a result of document analysis.

The stages of fieldwork may be as follows:

- initial identification of a research problem, research questions and a research sample,

- initial visit to the studied area carried out in order to clarify the research assumptions,
- development of the final research program, taking into account the research methods and tools to be used,
- data collection and analysis,
- summary of research results, formulation of conclusions and recommendations.

Additional interesting considerations concerning fieldwork are presented in (Patton 2015).

One of the basic, previously mentioned methods used within fieldwork is observation, which may have the following types: hidden or explicit (evaluators may be explicit or hide their intentions), structured or unstructured, direct or indirect, participant or non-participant.

An explicit observation is usually burdened with errors resulting from the unnatural attitudes and behavior of stakeholders, who know that they are being watched and that their statements are recorded and are subject to analysis. Hidden observation eliminates this drawback resulting from the explicit collection of data.

Structuring the observation means using tools systematizing the observation, such as questionnaires, a plan of implemented activities, guidelines and so on. The results of structured observation can lead to quantitative data. The unstructured form of observation also assumes activities related to the developed evaluation plan, but the research is conducted more flexibly, which sometimes results in low repeatability of research results and inconsistency of the results of research carried out by various evaluators.

Direct observation consists of the collection of data directly by the evaluator, and indirect observation is similar to relying on secondary data (data may come, for example, from evaluation reports for previous periods of project implementation, from analogous reports, projects already completed, etc.).

Participant observation assumes the collection of data as a result of the active functioning of the evaluator in the studied environment and among the project stakeholders—as one of them. Therefore, it is an observation from inside the project environment, which is also direct observation (the evaluator gathers data independently) and hidden observation at the same time. For example, an expert evaluating a training project may, for example, act as a training participant and thus examine its quality.

Participant observation is an opportunity to visualize the actual phase of project implementation. Hiding the researcher's intentions facilitates the obtaining of data that cannot be collected using other qualitative research methods, such as interviews and surveys. Therefore, it can be an important supplement in the evaluation process based on the use of many methods, and is also in accordance with the concept of integration of quantitative and qualitative methods.

Entering the environments of the researched projects and observing them from the inside allows better understanding of the existing problems that may be overcome thanks to the implementation of the projects. Meeting people in their natural conditions of life and professional activity promotes better understanding of their problems and motives for making specific decisions. Evaluators can flexibly adjust the time of conducted research and possibly increase the group of observed project stakeholders, depending on the needs identified on a regular basis.

Conducting field investigation requires (Babbie 2008):

- preparation after conducting background research, clarifying contact and relationship with subjects,
- conducting in-depth interviews, which are more demanding than interviews related to survey research (much less structured, less focused on gaining specific information, requiring patient, attentive and active listening),
- creating focus groups in order to zoom in on the analyzed problems and explore them more closely,
- accurate recording of the test results on an ongoing basis or doing it immediately after completing the research, to reflect all details.

4.3   Logic Models

Logic models (aka logical frameworks, project matrix or program/project theory) support two key evaluator challenges: measuring expected and achieved project outcomes as well as attributing those outcomes to specific project activities, thanks to the application of theory-based approaches (theory-driven evaluation) using theory of change (Treasury Board of Canada 2012). Theory of action and theory of change create a project theory that is a specific model or an explicit theory about project contributions to chains of intermediate results, as well as finally observed outcomes and impacts (Funnell and Rogers 2011).

Logic models are based on a systems approach and used by funders, project managers and evaluators to present (usually in graphic form) key assumptions and sequences of 'if-then' (causal) relationships of actions leading to desired outcomes and impacts of projects. They can be applied during planning and project implementation and explain logical relationships between main project elements, such as current situation (problems), resources (inputs), activities, outputs, outcomes and impacts. A clear illustration of these relationships supports understanding of cause-effect relationships linking existing problems needed to be overcome, implemented projects (resources involved, activities, outputs), outcomes and impacts achieved at the end-of-project realization (Fig. 4.1).

Approaches based on logic models and program theory were developed for the United States Agency for International Development in the late 1960s. For over half a century, such theories and approaches have been used mainly for planning, building design and the evaluation of temporary and unique activities such as international projects, European projects, development projects, public projects and others. These approaches support the determination of activities planned to solve identified existing problems and the specifications of objectives, as well as project results and reducing the risk of project failure.

Logic models have a universal character and are useful in the planning and implementation of projects of extremely different character. Earlier in this book it has already been mentioned that the European Commission

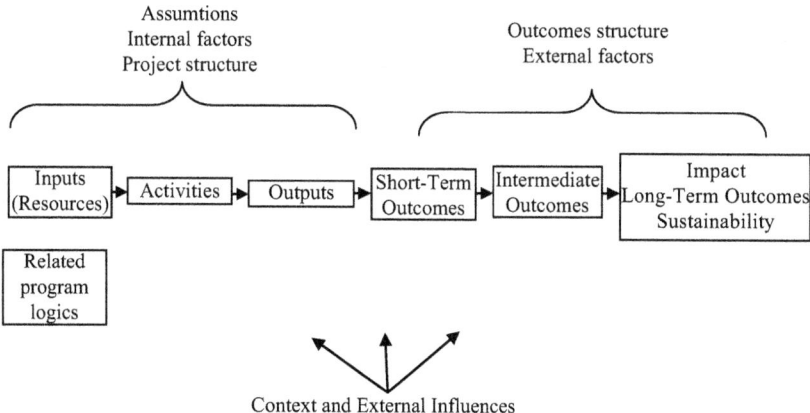

Fig. 4.1 Basic logic model. (Source: Based on Wholey et al. (2010))

recommends the parallel use of the Project Cycle Management (PCM) methodology and the Logical Framework Approach (LFA) which is based on the Logframe Logical Framework Matrix (LFM). LFA results from the experience gathered from various scientific management approaches: Results-Based Management (RBM), Goal Oriented Project Planning (GOPP), Objectives Oriented Project Planning (OOPP), Results Chain, Causality, Continuous Improvement Management and others.

The PCM methodological approach for supporting project management uses the cyclical nature of projects and concretizes the stages related to their preparation and implementation. The clear picture obtained from logic models makes it easier to build project management systems to monitor and evaluate them. According to the PCM methodology, identifying and formulating projects as a preparatory stage for their implementation is essential. LFA allows the effective support of the implementation of this stage and is also useful in all stages of the PCM cycle.

LFA can be defined as a process involving analyses: context, project stakeholders, problems, objectives, strategy and project logic with the use of LFM. For example, a logframe can take the form of a formalized matrix (table) with four columns and four (sometimes more) rows (Fig. 4.2). LFM supports project structuring and causal analysis, building project design and facilitating the organizing of its logical meaning, objectives, resources and logical chain of intended results.

Causal analysis is based on context study and research regarding the relationships between the identified needs and problems, their causes and some expected solutions. It helps to formulate a theory of change that planned and realized projects would like to try to achieve, and can involve

Project Description	Objectively verifiable indicators	Sources of verification	Assumption
Impact			
Outcomes			
Outputs - Results			
Activities	Inputs		
			Pre-conditions

Fig. 4.2 Typical form of a LFM. (Source: Based on Project Cycle Management Guidelines (2004))

diverse approaches, methods and techniques, for example, stakeholder analysis, SWOT analysis, feasibility studies, community mapping, problem trees/solution tree analysis, objective trees and others.

A logic model is built in the following stages (Wholey et al. 2010):

1. gathering the relevant information (interviewing people, analyzing documents, observing changing contexts),
2. context and stakeholder analysis, identifying problems and needs the project will solve, causal analysis and objectives analysis,
3. designing the elements of the logic model in a matrix (table),
4. drawing up the logic model, developing the model diagram and building project design,
5. verifying the model with stakeholders,
6. application of the built model to performance measurement and evaluation.

After accomplishment of the stage of gathering relevant information, a context and stakeholder analysis is performed. Stakeholders can have different impacts on project implementation and there are many types of classification of these. One of the examples of classifications results from the different meanings that stakeholders place on their relationships with projects (e.g. stakeholders: main, secondary). There may also be a division into internal stakeholders (involved in project implementation) or external stakeholders (subject to the positive or negative impact of particular projects), as well as the division into stakeholders having a positive influence on the implementation of a sequence of project activities or having a negative impact on achieving its goals (impeding the performance of this sequence of activities).

The results of context and stakeholder analysis are the starting point for the preparation of the justification for the implementation of the project, containing the identification of problems and needs (faced by specific target groups) the project will solve. Identification of existing problems that must be resolved is a prerequisite for the implementation of each project and it is necessary to find justification for the implementation of projects in the form of benefits resulting from solving these problems. The result of the problems analysis is to present in a concise and readable form the current negative situation: the reason for which the project is to be implemented. Lack of clear and strong justification of the current negative situation makes it impossible to move to the analysis of project objectives.

Problem analysis can be carried out using a problem tree by characterizing an existing negative situation justifying the need for corrective activities, defining the basic problems faced by some potential target groups of the project, and carrying out a causal analysis of problems that have been completed.

The analysis of the existing situation, negative phenomena and problems of the potential target group should be carried out with the active participation of as many stakeholders as possible. As a result of discussions, with their participation, the essence of problems and proposed solutions should be determined. The identified problem should reflect the existing negative situation that can be changed as a result of the planned project implementation. Usually, there is not only one problem, but a group of problems related to a cause-effect relationship. Therefore, a tree of problems is a useful tool for conducting such analyses and presenting their results (Fig. 4.3).

The negative situation justifies the intervention in the form of the implemented project and it can be assigned the desired situation which

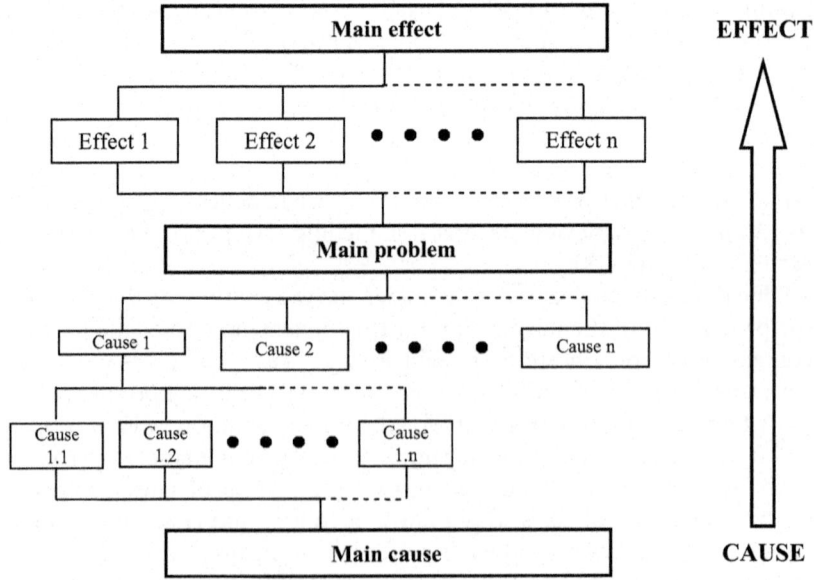

Fig. 4.3   Example of a problem tree. (Source: Based on Project Cycle Management Guidelines (2004))

will probably occur in the future, on condition that certain activities are implemented. An objective tree can be used to create a type of graphical visualization (forecast) of this future desired situation. Building such a tree involves characterizing the desired situation in the future, determining possible realizable activities and changing negative factors (occurring in the form of problems) into positive ones (the possibility of achieving the sequence of activity objectives).

After identifying the objectives and preparing the objectives tree, one must specify how to achieve these objectives using the chosen strategy. The choice of strategy should take into account the results of previous objectives analysis, in addition to the internal and external conditions of the project implementation. By 'internal conditions' is understood, for example, the knowledge and experience of people involved in the project implementation, the organizational capabilities of the project contractor, the resources owned by him/her and so on. The external conditions of the project implementation are, for example, the project implementation environment, its stakeholders, budget, time for implementation and so on. Therefore, for example, there may be a lack of resources (including financial resources) or time to perform all planned activities and achieve the related results and objectives.

The identified objectives and strategies for achieving these allow for the implementation of the stage concerning drawing up the logic model, developing the model diagram and building the project design. In individual rows of the table, for example, (looking from the bottom to the top of the table), activities, results, outcomes and impacts can be recorded. Building project design and utilizing LFM often runs in a rather unusual way. The assumptions written in the last column are the first values entered in the process of filling in this logic matrix. The typical logic of reading is moving from right to left, and the content of each row is entered from the bottom to the top. There are two basic LFM logics: vertical and horizontal. The first assumes reading and filling the table using rows, while the second is focused on the columns. It is also possible to use Zig-Zag Logic, which assumes the filling of the table from the bottom to the top, starting from the pre-conditions in the right bottom cell (Project Cycle Management Guidelines 2004).

The second LFM column may contain the objectively verifiable indicators, which at the beginning are generally identified, and then are specified in accordance with the target group and in compliance with the QQT (Quantity, Quality and Time) principle (Andler 2011). Indicators take into account the location parameters and are used to measure the partial results of projects and their advancement levels in achieving the set objectives. They allow the measurement (verification) of progress and project efficiency, and therefore should be determined in operationally measurable units.

While working on filling the second column containing the objectively verifiable indicators, one should take into account the sources of data and information necessary to carry out the verification (third column). It should contain a list of verification sources. The indicators should not be entered in the LFM, the use of which is unrealistic from the point of view of the amount of time devoted to it, the incurring of financial outlays, the contribution of the people involved and so on.

The third column should contain a list of not only sources of data for verification, but also a description of relatively simple ways of obtaining this data. Indicators that are problematic to use, due to the difficulty of access to sources of information and data, should be removed. The basis for the decision to delete a given indicator may be, for example, too-complex an algorithm of data collection, large estimated costs of gathering information, huge work expenses and so on. The description of information sources in the third column should also include the specification of persons responsible for collecting information for verification, the schedule for conducting this activity and the format of recording data.

The completed model, after entering the data into table cells, should be verified after consultations conducted with the participation of stakeholders. In this case, it is possible to use the constructed model in performance measurement and evaluation efficiently.

4.4   NEW QUALITATIVE INTELLIGENT SYSTEMS

Inductive reasoning associated with qualitative analyses with the use of intelligent systems begins in a typical way for qualitative research, that is, from empirical research and specific observations aimed at obtaining a saved collection of data, information and empirical knowledge concerning a concrete project reality that is subject to evaluation. Based on this collection, the discovery of patterns and regularities is made and this allows the building of another form of knowledge, which one should carefully explore and consequently reach some general conclusions about the evaluated reality and project.

As a result of conducting evaluation studies, more and more data are obtained, which (if they are of a qualitative nature) are to some extent immediately analyzed in a parallel way. Paradoxically, the significant technological possibilities of collecting data obtained, for example, as a result of observation, in practice make their rational use impossible. Reference in project evaluation processes only to some experts and the possibilities of simultaneous collecting and parallel analyzing of qualitative data become unrealistic. Supporting the work of experts by the use of conventional information systems with larger and larger databases often intensifies problems related to the appropriate use of increasing amounts of data. Out of necessity, experts use only a small part of the data, information and knowledge from the resources they have.

A significant challenge for modern evaluation has been building and using intelligent systems that support and actively advice experts who collect and analyze qualitative data. Such systems should not only support the analysis of available qualitative data, but also be characterized by machine intelligence as a result of discovering knowledge from data that can be observed subjectively, suggesting specific decision rules, adapting to a particular project situation and the specific needs of researchers and evaluators.

As for the range of qualitative data, the systems should be wide enough and include not only an unordered or nominal date obtained as a result of subjective observations, but should also deal with the exploration of written and multimedia resources available online. Useful technologies are primarily inductive reasoning and data mining for knowledge discovering, and text mining, web mining, image and video processing for pattern recognition. Knowledge discovery conducted within the framework of qualitative research, by using machine learning and in accordance with inductive reasoning, leads to the detection of patterns and generalizations for example, in the form of algebraic equations, logical expressions, programs, semantic networks, graphs, decision trees, decision and association rules.

As part of interdisciplinary methodological research on evaluation systems related to qualitative research, systems with rule-based knowledge bases, processing methods of uncertain information and machine learning should be developed. In rule-based systems, reasoning involves drawing conclusions by induction, and this induction process is implemented in the evaluation system on the basis of machine learning examples. In processes of inductive reasoning and supporting decision-making, generalizations are obtained as a result of the analysis of known sets of projects with common features.

Supporting decisions can be made using interdisciplinary data mining and analytics processes of discovering hidden patterns in large sets, involving methods drawn from computer science, machine learning, AI, statistics, discrete mathematics and others. Generally, the process of knowledge discovery in data mining can be, for example, as follows (Sheng 2017):

- data selection (from database to target data),
- pre-processing (data cleaning, collecting required information, dealing with redundant and missing data),
- transformation (conversion of data into the desired format compatible with a specific method of data mining),
- data mining (pattern discovery processes),
- assessing (making decisions on the relevance and sufficiency of discovered patterns for building knowledge representation in current contexts).

In evaluation processes using qualitative research systems, two knowledge discovery modeling mechanisms should be used in parallel: data-driven, based on data mining and knowledge-driven, based on human expert knowledge. The usefulness of this hybrid approach is confirmed in research regarding real-world classification applications; these two types of knowledge are typically independent as well as complementary (Lianmeng et al. 2016).

Qualitative evaluation systems based on knowledge can be generally divided into two types: supervised learning (based on examples from training sets) and implementing unsupervised learning processes. Thanks to learning systems, it is realizable to discover useful knowledge in project evaluation processes. Recording this knowledge in the form of rules is tantamount to creating so-called symbolic knowledge representation.

In the case of supervised learning (in pattern taxonomy models), the rules are induced on the basis of the examples from the training sets, while unsupervised learning processes assume the use of a non-pattern taxonomy and these are primarily association models. Discovering relationships, correlations and associations occupies an important place in data mining and is useful in the processes of modeling and implementation of the project evaluation system.

Association rules can be generated using the selected machine learning algorithm resulting from the use of a particular AI method. This interdisciplinary field of knowledge is very extensive and involves research in many areas: computer science, mathematics, logic, biology, neurology, psychology, management and others.

Qualitative evaluation systems based on knowledge can have the ability to learn, adapt and self-improve thanks to the acquired empirical knowledge about evaluated projects. This knowledge may come from experts or from other people (e.g. program and project stakeholders), and using one of the available knowledge presentation methods it can be saved in knowledge bases, which are the basic elements of many intelligent and knowledge-based systems.

The rule-based system provides clear and symbolic knowledge representation of a qualitative character. This method of knowledge representation enables the relatively simple implementation of an interactive user dialogue with this type of system. Decisions suggested by rule systems can be reasonably justified with the help of selected rules that are understandable for average users.

A typical knowledge representation in the form of a rule constitutes the following conditional sentence: 'if {collection of project evaluation criteria} – to {set of decision attributes}'. This rule reflects the relationships occurring in empirical data and the subjective opinions expressed by experts evaluating projects, depending on their knowledge, experience and attitudes, as well as the specifics of evaluated projects, existing socioeconomic phenomena and their environment.

Both symbolic and rule knowledge representation have a number of advantages, the most important of which is a clear and understandable way of presenting the saved knowledge. This knowledge representation method enables easy understanding of the sense of a conditional sentence in the form: if a condition, then a decision. Therefore, for the evaluators, a uniform, explicit, legible and practical interpretation of the obtained qualitative research results is provided, for example, regarding the analysis of the project stakeholders' opinions. This is particularly important from the point of view of qualitative research of often contradictory and subjective opinions, for example, from interviews and observations.

The acquired empirical qualitative data could not be processed using classical numerical algorithms, and this is possible in the case of rule-based systems that may use reasoning mechanisms functioning in an intelligent way which is intuitively understandable to people. In addition, rule systems are characterized by good implementation capabilities and relatively easy scalability in the case of the need to expand knowledge bases, which is implemented relatively simply: by adding new rules to already existing knowledge bases.

In the case of using supervised learning, pattern taxonomy models are built according to discriminative models (conditional models) and rules for building knowledge bases are induced on the basis of examples from training sets, for which specific classifications are known. At the output of qualitative evaluation rule-based systems, the resulting knowledge is obtained, ensuing from patterns (rules) extracted from training sets.

The rules generated in the learning processes define the decision classes for new projects and enable the desired classification to be achieved. The project evaluation process may be based on the assignment of new projects, described by means of evaluation criteria, to one of the defined decision classes. The existence of these classes is determined a priori, that is, on the principle of assumption. As a result of project sorting, they can be assigned to individual decision classes.

Knowledge recorded in project evaluation systems can be updated thanks to iteratively repeated learning processes, which are implemented in a manner resulting from the adopted knowledge representation method, and among these an important place is occupied by methods based on mathematical inspirations and the use of extensions, as well as certain generalizations of classical mathematics accepting gradation of values and unclear assignment to specific sets.

The best-known approaches inspired by mathematics are based on two theories: fuzzy set theory (Zadeh 1965) and rough set theory (Pawlak 1991). Both theories assume gradation of values, departures from classic set theory and the possibility of occurrence of many-valued logic, which means giving up the approach allowing only true or false conclusions. In this case it is assumed that the element can only 'partly' belong to the set. An important advantage of both theories is the ability to create the basis for the implementation of qualitative systems useful in the processing of data obtained experimentally under conditions of uncertainty. These theories are also useful in practical applications related to the creation of knowledge representation in learning systems used in qualitative data analysis and project classification.

Fuzzy set theory is better known in the world due to its earlier creation. The second of these theories was presented later; it is complementary to the first one and is the effect of research on some logical characteristics of information systems (information tables). Such tables may contain a description of the evaluated projects in the form of a set of evaluation criteria (Table 4.1).

Table 4.1   Decision table for knowledge representation about projects

Projects	Criterion c_1	Criterion c_2	...	Criterion c_m	Decision
x_1	$f(x_1, c_1)$	$f(x_1, c_2)$	...	$f(x_1, c_m)$	d_1
x_2	$f(x_2, c_1)$	$f(x_2, c_2)$	...	$f(x_2, c_m)$	d_2
...	...	...	...	...	
x_n	$f(x_n, c_1)$	$f(x_n, c_2)$	...	$f(x_n, c_m)$	d_n

Source: Based on Grzeszczyk (2017)

Projects from training sets stored in a decision table with project evaluation criteria and a decision attribute create in this way the initial representation of symbolic knowledge, which is subject to modifications as a result of the implementation of learning processes. The effect of this kind of processes is a set of generated rules, which are useful for classifying new projects not previously saved in the system.

The basic concept associated with rough set theory is approximation, which enables the representation and processing of vague concepts. To describe each of these kinds of concepts, two approximations (sharp concepts) called lower and upper approximations are necessary.

Figure 4.4 depicts the line specifying an exemplary shape of rough set that runs in an area referred to as a boundary region. It is an area reflecting a sort of indeterminacy and uncertainty.

Uncertain data, information and knowledge modeling are enabled by intelligent granular computing systems. Granular computing approaches are applied for information processing and complex problem-solving via multiple levels of granularity (Gong et al. 2017). The ease of building a granular information structure, the simplicity of knowledge representation for the implementation of rules knowledge bases useful in practical applications determines the choice of one of the methods for representing information and knowledge about projects. In the case of rough sets, the granules of information describing the so-called universe (the reality associated with the evaluated projects) are the smallest (in other words: basic, atomic) elements of the characteristic of a given set X belonging to this universe If the given set X cannot be represented in the form of the sum of granules of information, then it is a rough set, and granular approximations are used.

Data, information and knowledge regarding evaluated projects are granular in nature because the evaluation criteria assume a finite number

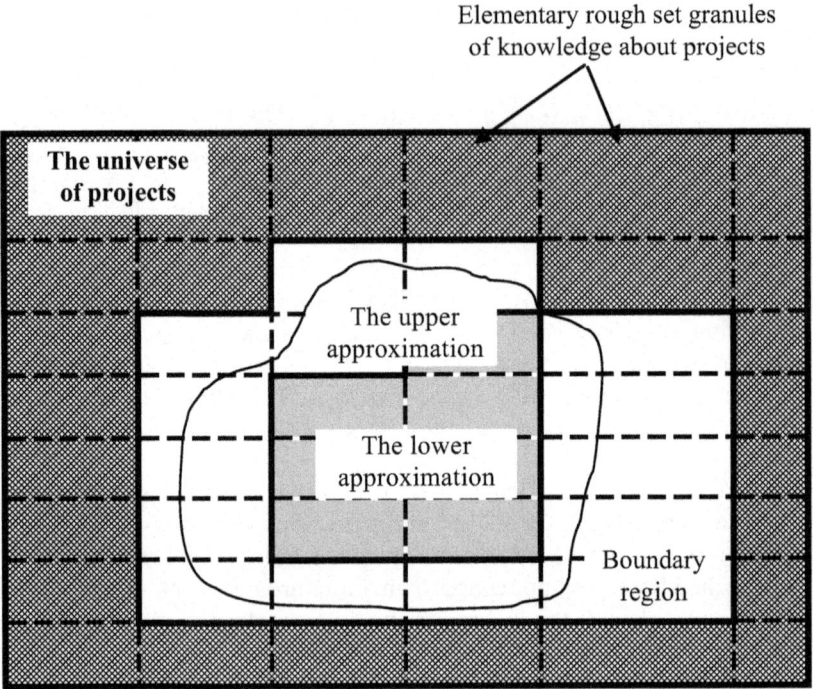

Fig. 4.4 Project evaluation and granular computing. (Source: Based on Pawlak (1991) and Grzeszczyk (2013))

of acceptable values. Depending on the necessity, by increasing the number of granules, the accuracy of the evaluation is improved. For example, instead of three grains (good, bad, to be corrected), one can also add grains: very good, very bad, to improve the accuracy of the evaluation to the level of five granules.

Granules of knowledge regarding qualitative evaluation research can be saved in the project evaluation system, for example, using rough sets. Multi-criterial analysis using generalized rough set theory provides an opportunity to ensure the proper accuracy of defining fuzzy terms in a knowledge-based evaluation system. Lower and upper approximations can be built up from granules of knowledge. The accuracy of defining a vague concept improves as the number of evaluation criteria describing individual projects increases. The values of these criteria can be saved in the form of an information table.

It should be noted that the foundation on which the Classical Rough Sets Approach (CRSA [Pawlak 1991], also called Pawlak Sets) is based, is Indiscernibility Relations (hence the other name of this theory: Indiscernibility-based Rough Sets) to distinguish it from generalized rough sets developed under many research trends. The most important advantages of CRSA are:

- good application opportunities resulting from the use of knowledge granules,
- relatively simple mathematical description and easy implementation using IT,
- the algorithms designed and implemented are usually relatively not particularly complex, efficient and quick,
- a clear form of calculation results in the form of decision rules, simplifying their interpretation,
- significant tolerance for inconsistencies and missing data,
- the ease of modifying the theory for better suitability for specific applications,
- the possibility of applying this theory in the processes of knowledge discovery in empirical data stored in readable decision tables,
- the ease of processing data, information and knowledge gained empirically (quantitative and qualitative),
- usefulness in the processes of socio-economic data analysis, which are poorly structured and fuzzy,
- the ability to eliminate redundant data, information and knowledge,
- ease of reducing the number of generated decision rules, recorded in the knowledge base and the limitation of computer-intensive calculations.

In the processes of solving multi-criteria problems useful in the qualitative evaluation of projects, the trend generalizing rough sets using dominance relation is useful. This methodical trend is based on the application of the dominance relation, compliant with the Pareto approach (Pareto dominance relation) (Greco et al. 2001; Blaszczynski et al. 2007). When using it, it is possible to perform a relatively objective multi-criteria sorting process in which projects described in the values of evaluation criteria are compared. A Dominance-based Rough Sets Approach (DRSA) is used to solve typical multi-criterial decision problems, that is, ranking, selection, sorting and others (Greco et al. 1999).

An important advantage of the DRSA methodical approach is the relative ease of obtaining practical applications and the possibility of implementing these using IT technology. Using this trend, the examples (project evaluation criteria) that learn the system can be entered into the decision table rows (similarly to CRSA). The evaluation criteria describing the evaluated projects are in turn ordered according to preferences compliant with the DRSA approach.

When building qualitative evaluation systems based on knowledge, it is possible to use scientific achievements resulting from CRSA applications and research work on the development of this theory toward DRSA. The basic feature of the DRSA trend is the replacement of the conception of integration of set approximations and indiscernibility relations with the idea of combining set approximations and dominance relations. This is particularly useful when solving a multi-criteria problem of project evaluation. The DRSA trend requires the use of attributes describing evaluated objects that have a preferentially ordered domain, as in the case of project evaluation criteria. The requirement for the existence of pre-determined and preferably ordered decision classes to which decisions related to particular objects (in this case evaluated projects) are assigned is also met for project evaluation problems.

For both theories, CRSA and DRSA, there is a division between the attributes describing the evaluated objects for the conditional (for DRSA these are evaluation criteria) and for the decision-making attributes, usually stored in the decision table. There should be a semantic correlation between these attributes, in accordance with the dominance principle. As a result, the decision rules generated on the basis of the decision table reflect the dependencies and relationships that exist between conditional attributes (criteria) and decision-making attributes, taking into account the dominance principle (Słowiński et al. 2002).

The newer trend of DRSA on the one hand is characterized by the more important advantages of the classic CRSA approach, that is, it enables data analysis (under risk and uncertainty conditions) related to solving the problems of classification (sorting into predefined decision classes), ordering (ranking of options) and selection of objects. On the other hand, it is also a practically useful approach, applicable to the process of supporting multi-criteria decisions, for example, project evaluation.

The project evaluation process is based on many preferentially ordered criteria.

Data analysis consistent with the DRSA trend leads to the generation of decision rules taking into account the preferential relationships occurring in these data. The knowledge base built from the decision-making rules reflects the model of preferences discovered from empirical data that may come from both data-driven processes and knowledge-driven processes based on human expert knowledge. Such a knowledge base may be useful in the process of classifying new projects that have not been used in the processes of the evaluation of system learning and generating decision rules.

REFERENCES

Andler, N. (2011). *Tools for Project Management. Workshops and Consulting: A Must-Have Compendium of Essential Tools and Techniques.* Erlangen, Germany: Publicis Publishing.

Babbie, E. R. (2008). *The Basics of Social Research.* Belmont, USA: Wadsworth Publishing Company.

Blaszczynski, J., Greco, S., & Slowinski, R. (2007). Multi-Criteria Classification – A New Scheme for Application of Dominance-Based Decision Rules. *European Journal of Operational Research, 181*(3/September): 1030–1044.

Funnell, S. C., & Rogers, P. J. (2011). Introduction. In S. C. Funnell & P. J. Rogers (Eds.), *Purposeful Program Theory: Effective Use of Theories of Change and Logic Models.*San Francisco: Jossey-Bass, John Wiley & Sons Imprint.

Gong, F., Shao, M. W., & Qiu, G. (2017, April). Concept Granular Computing Systems and Their Approximation Operators. *International Journal of Machine Learning and Cybernetics, 8*(2), 627–640.

Greco, S., Matarazzo, B., & Słowinski, R. (1999). Chapter 14. The Use of Rough Sets and Fuzzy Sets in MCDM. In T. Gal, T. Stewart, & T. Hanne (Eds.), *Advances in Multiple Criteria Decision Making.* Boston: Kluwer Academic Publishers.

Greco, S., Matarazzo, B., & Słowiński, R. (2001). Rough Set Theory for Multicriteria Decision Analysis. *European Journal of Operational Research, 129*(1), 1–47.

Grzeszczyk, T. A. (2013). *Towards the Model of Comprehensive Project Evaluation System.* Warsaw: Faculty of Management, Warsaw University of Technology.

Grzeszczyk, T. A. (2017). *Rough Rule-Based Systems for Sparse and Dense Data Analysis Used in Project Evaluation* (Vol. 31). 4th International Conference on Management Science and Management Innovation. Advances in Economics, Business and Management Research.

Lianmeng, J., Thierry, D., & Quan, P. (2016). A Hybrid Belief Rule-Based Classification System Based on Uncertain Training Data and Expert Knowledge. *IEEE Transactions on Systems Man Cybernetics-Systems, 46*(12), 1711–1723.

Martin, W. E., & Bridgmon, K. D. (2012). *Quantitative and Statistical Research Methods: From Hypothesis to Results.* San Francisco: Jossey-Bass, John Wiley & Sons Imprint.

Patton, M. Q. (2002). *Qualitative Research & Evaluation Methods.* Thousand Oaks/London/New Delhi: SAGE Publications Inc.

Patton, M. Q. (2015). *Qualitative Research & Evaluation Methods. Integrating Theory and Practice.* Thousand Oaks/London/New Delhi: SAGE Publications Inc.

Pawlak, Z. (1991). *Rough Sets. Theoretical Aspects of Reasoning About Data.* Dordrecht: Kluwer.

Project Cycle Management Guidelines. (2004). *Aid Delivery Methods.* Brussels: European Commission – EuropeAid Cooperation Office.

Russ-Eft, D., & Preskill, H. (2009). *Evaluation in Organizations: A Systematic Approach to Enhancing Learning. Performance and Change.* New York: Basic Books.

Sheng, T. W. (2017). *Knowledge Discovery Using Pattern Taxonomy Model in Text Mining* (PhD Dissertation). Faculty of Information Technology, Queensland University of Technology.

Słowiński, R., Greco, S., & Matarazzo, B. (2002). Axiomatization of Utility, Outranking and Decision-Rule Preference Models for Multiple-Criteria Classification Problems Under Partial Inconsistency with the Dominance Principle. *Control and Cybernetics, 31,* 1005–1035.

Stawarski, C., & Phillips, P. P. (2008). *Data Collection: Planning for and Collecting All Types of Data.* San Francisco: Pfeiffer, John Wiley & Sons Imprint.

Treasury Board of Canada. (2012). *Theory-Based Approaches to Evaluation: Concepts and Practices.*

Wholey, J. S., Hatry, H. P., & Newcomer, K. E. (2010). *Handbook of Practical Program Evaluation.* San Francisco: Jossey-Bass, John Wiley & Sons Imprint.

Zadeh, L. A. (1965). Fuzzy Sets. *Information and Control, 8*(3), 338–353.

CHAPTER 5

Principles of Integrated Evaluation Systems

Abstract This chapter provides philosophical and theoretical considerations, mainly regarding new paradigms, systems approaches and Integral Theory useful for further modeling of mixed intelligent systems. The application of systems approaches makes it possible to build holistic and comprehensive models of evaluated projects. The author proposes the need to conduct research leading toward new paradigms to be introduced in the evaluation field. Integral Theory enables the methodological pluralism essential for the introduction of mixed systems studies, as well as building holistic understanding, multidisciplinary and complex management and project evaluation fields, combining many perspectives, methodologies and meta-paradigm approach into a single coherent vision. To solve a complicated problem of building a model of the comprehensive project evaluation system, one should search using quantitative-qualitative systems approaches and integral theory of project evaluation, alongside innovative approaches to evaluation based on concepts from computational intelligence methods.

Keywords Evaluation approaches and methods • Paradigms in evaluation • Systems approaches • Integral Theory in evaluation

5.1   PHILOSOPHICAL CONSIDERATIONS

The reflections presented in this section concern the need for continuing a discussion on alternative philosophical ideas and pluralism of approaches in evaluation research development. Understanding selected aspects related to different philosophical ideas enables efficient transition to work on paradigms (fundamental assumptions about reality), which are the basis for the use of approaches, methods and systems for project evaluation (Table 5.1).

According to interdisciplinary integration, paradigms (worldviews) practical in evaluation processes should reflect specific concepts, philosophical assumptions, theories, ways of thinking, research approaches, methods and standards typical for selected scientific areas, in addition to representing universal values, useful across multiple disciplines. Among philosophical assumptions in evaluation paradigms the following can be distinguished above all: axiology (study of value), ontology (nature of being, existence and reality), epistemology (nature of knowledge) and methodology (theoretical analysis of research methods) (Mertens and Wilson 2012).

It is worth pursuing philosophical considerations of a vast and multifaceted nature, although for simplicity, only a few philosophical trends can be mentioned here. Among the major ones, the following can be highlighted above all: positivism, objectivism, constructivism, realism, interpretivism and pragmatism.

The trend of positivism is characteristic of the quantitative-systemic approach and it assumes the possibility of obtaining objective and valid knowledge about the evaluated project reality through systematic research based largely on quantitative scientific methods (Royse et al. 2010). Such studies allow the discovery of many dependencies that combine input resources with project effects and their generalization. Applied models lead to a significant simplification of described reality and they do not take into account the hard to measure, multifaceted input resources, diversity of projects and their effects. In turn, objectivists believe that objective truth exists, and can be assessed in isolation from the influences, feelings, attitudes and private opinions of some evaluators, as well as that reality is independent from researchers.

Due to the need to consider not only quantitative and simplified models of the evaluated reality in research, one should also draw inspiration from other philosophical trends, which reject the abovementioned

Table 5.1 Philosophies, approaches and methods

Philosophies		Paradigms in evaluation (interdisciplinary integration)	Methodologies	Approaches		Methods, models and systems
Positivism, objectivism	Empirical data, determinism and scientific methods		Hard systems methodology	Deductive, top-down	If some premises are true, then conclusions are certainly true	Quantitative
Constructivism, interpretivism	Multiple values, interactions and perspectives		Soft systems methodology	Inductive, bottom-up	If some premises are true, then conclusions are probably true	Qualitative
Pragmatism, transformativism	Pluralistic methodology, real-world problem solving		Mixed intelligent systems	Abductive	Explanatory reasoning, conclusions are guesses	System of methods, mixed methods, mixed intelligent systems

limitations to a large extent. Constructivists reject the possibility of objective knowledge existence and are closer to the idea of not only a quantitative, but also a qualitative and multidimensional evaluation, which allows taking greater account of the multidimensionality and comprehensiveness of the assessed phenomena and problems. The supporters of this philosophical trend believe that in the evaluation of phenomena, a key role is played by the researchers who have their own theories enabling them to find a way to better understand the reality under investigation. In this situation, constructivists are close to qualitative methods, models and systems, in which data are collected by observers and simultaneously analyzed according to their theories.

According to the constructivist philosophy, project evaluators and stakeholders are at the heart of the research process, and they are the primary source of qualitative data, information and knowledge. In case of significant diversity of stakeholder groups and divergences of their views, evaluators take an interactive, responsive and orchestrated approach and explore the qualitative data obtained in order to find compromise results (Tavistock Institute 2003).

Constructivists are less focused on quantitative research and theories that allow accurate measurement of the phenomena studied. They fully understand that the evaluation of projects requires taking into account many levels, interdependencies and effects that are qualitative and difficult to measure. In fact, there are interactive relations between project evaluators and stakeholders that occur in various configurations and are involved in project-related processes, which usually have an immeasurable and qualitative nature. According to this approach, the evaluation process should take into account different points of view, attitudes, cultural and psychological conditions and other non-measurable factors. The evaluation report should be based mainly on the subjective opinions of evaluators, resulting from contacts with many stakeholders and not based on the results of quantitative models, which may be considered reliable, precise and objective in some scientific communities (Bachtler and Wren 2006).

Similar to constructivism, the philosophical trend of realism is in contrast to positivist assumptions and does not allow for the discovery of generalized and objective knowledge through quantitative research. In scientific study, according to the philosophical trend of realism, it is assumed that the assessed reality has an objective or independent existence that is not perceived by an observer (Royse et al. 2010). In such research processes, the focus is on discovering complex and comprehensive socio-economic and environmental mechanisms within the framework of policies, strategies, programs and their links with the evaluated projects (Pawson and Tilley 2004). Such processes of discovering knowledge about the mechanisms and causes of changes, as well as learning about the socio-economic and environmental dimensions of projects, are compared to opening and exploring the contents of 'black boxes' (Astbury and Leeuw 2010).

In the case of realism approach, thematic evaluations and multidimensional in-depth case studies have fundamental importance, during which multifaceted effects resulting from the interaction between participants and project stakeholders are estimated (Tavistock Institute 2003). In principle, the trend of realism can be classified among those that place the main emphasis on evaluation studies of a multifaceted nature, close to qualitative research. However, they do not reject quantitative models, and on a scale on which in extremely opposite places positivism and interpretivism are located, it can be placed somewhere between these.

Interpretivism is a type of epistemology highlighting the specificity of conducting research among people who are 'social actors' playing their roles on the scenes of human life, and whose behaviors can be interpreted in different ways according to the accepted set of evaluation criteria. In interpretivist epistemologies an empathetic attitude of evaluators is assumed, entering the world of the evaluated actors and objective implementing interpretation processes from their point of view (Saunders et al. 2007).

Interpretivism provides a philosophical basis for qualitative research, while an alternative trend is pragmatism, which is related to interventions, actions and constructive knowledge (Goldkuhl 2012). Pragmatism states a unique philosophical worldview as it highlights the nature of experiences (not the nature of reality), focuses on outcomes of actions (instead of nature of truth questions) and considers shared beliefs (in place of research regarding isolated, individual sources of beliefs) (Patton 2015). This philosophical trend provides the meta-methodology, offers pluralism in opposition to philosophical dualism and justifies mixed methods and mixed systems approaches (Patton 2015).

Philosophical considerations results make it possible to start a discussion about new paradigm needs in the field of project management and evaluation development, and to focus on advanced types of qualitative and quantitative methods and mixed intelligent systems suitable for comprehensive evaluation.

5.2   The Need for New Paradigms in Evaluation

Years ago, in social and educational evaluation research it was possible to observe an increasing interest in quantitative approaches and a reliance on project evaluation models that did not consider qualitative variables sufficiently. Such approaches provide illusory belief in the modernity of research processes, and the accuracy and objectivity of the results obtained.

For over 40 years, M. Patton has been developing new paradigms and approaches in the field of evaluation, starting with the alternative paradigm based on human behavior meaning, subjective mental states understanding, social interactions contexts, qualitative approaches and methodology, as well as the involved and active role of the evaluation researcher (Patton 1975). He also emphasizes the uniqueness of creative evaluation research, which should proceed differently from studies conducted within the framework of various scientific disciplines and recognizes methodological flexibility and a wide range of worthwhile research approaches, systems and methods (Patton 1987).

The diversity of evaluated projects is so significant that it is doubtful whether a consensus on fundamental paradigms in evaluation can ever be reached. Paradigm debates should result in guidance on how to deal with the possibilities available in evaluation studies. Orthodox deliberations on the correctness and priority approach to particular paradigms should be replaced by discussion of a huge set of available approaches, systems and methods according to the paradigm of choices (Patton 2011).

Compatibility with the paradigm of choices means, among other aspects, the interdisciplinary character of evaluation studies. In developing project evaluation issues, it is necessary to use paradigms and achievements resulting from the development of modern social sciences, economic and management theory and to draw inspiration from the principles of intelligent learning organization, system approaches, new ICT technologies, learning systems and artificial intelligence. The research achievements on models of intelligent organizations and the ICT supporting them should therefore be a key source of inspiration for the further development of project evaluation systems.

The increasing usability of new information technologies in evaluation processes is necessary due to the increasing frequency of implementation of projects whose significance and objectives go beyond financial results. Currently, relatively few business projects are purely commercial in nature and in this case, it is possible to use a relatively small number of criteria, which are quantitative, legible and do not raise any doubts of interpretation. Previously, only in the case of public, development and European projects were the evaluation criteria characterized by considerable complexity and interpretative doubts. It is not advisable to limit oneself to simple financial indicator-based approaches, so multifaceted (quantitative and qualitative) researches, often taking into account the widely differing project objectives and stakeholder needs, are necessary. Therefore, the need to broaden the range of approaches and methods available arises.

In view of the fact that the results of the whole evaluation process depends mainly on the correctness of data collection and analysis, the methods and systems associated with them have fundamental importance. Data processing technologies and intelligent data science methods are crucial for the implementation of these processes. It is necessary to search for new intelligent fragmented methods inspired by advances in ICT, and to develop comprehensive systems based on the modification and combination of methods, as well as to build systems based on original proposals of mixed systems of multifaceted project evaluation.

Since project evaluation processes are increasingly driven by data, ensuring a proper way of data collection and analysis for the evaluation process is a major challenge. There are problems with Big Data applications: frequent inconsistencies and doubtful quality of structured data, as well as unstructured data. The existing literature in the field of Big Data and Data Science methods in project evaluation processes is not extensive (Olsson and Bull-Berg 2015), although it sets further directions for the development of evaluation methods and systems. In particular, the proposed solutions may be based on intelligent systems and technologies.

It is exceptionally important that a set of selected Data Science methods applicable for Big Data, using artificial intelligence methods, should be based on qualitative empirical data. The data processing in intelligent systems can be done in a similar way, based on knowledge gathered from experiences of expert evaluators. Knowledge-Based Systems, expert systems and Business Intelligences are known among these technologies, through which one can gather empirical evaluation knowledge. Intelligent algorithms based on AI methods can be used to extract knowledge from large collections of unstructured data sets and to discover data dependencies.

In the future, Big Data research, useful in the field of project evaluation, could lead to the formulation of the Big Data Paradigm. The knowledge-based economy paradigm and sustainable development paradigm, along with economic, social and technological aspects play an important role in this type of research. The Big Data paradigm primarily focuses on various aspects of evaluation decision support implemented under the conditions of generally formulated research assumptions. Compared to data mining and Business Intelligence approaches and systems, decisions are made through real-time processing directly on poorly structured source data and this paradigm is evidence of new ICT trends and data science analysis methods.

In the classical literature on business and management sciences one can see a view on the necessity of formulating new and fundamental paradigms enabling further development of the theory and practice of social science and management (Drucker 2001). The field of project management and evaluation also needs to undertake a paradigm change to meet the increasing demands connected with multifaceted and comprehensive nature of projects realized in a turbulent environment.

Evaluation is an overarching meta-discipline growing fast and combining fundamentals of social science insights, systems analysis, decision theory and multidisciplinary approaches (Picciotto 1999). Contemporary circumstances necessitate the development of this meta-discipline and, related to this, interdisciplinary scientific research undertaken by experts from different fields and increasingly sophisticated approaches for evaluation based on traditional evaluation paradigms and those resulting from development, for example, intelligent systems.

It may be useful to modify the traditional way of thinking about evaluation and link it with social sciences, above all. It is necessary to develop interdisciplinary approaches, closing gaps between scientific disciplines. New approaches and paradigms should make it easier to take into account the views of project stakeholders considering the larger amount (submitted by them) of quantitative and qualitative data collected during the pre-analysis research. This will allow evaluation studies to better reflect their needs and help build mutual trust between the evaluator and project stakeholders.

Modern approaches and paradigms related to the collection of large amounts of data, information and knowledge processing also facilitate the implementation of solutions compatible with a new evaluation culture and paradigms (related to operational, tactical and strategic levels) assuming frequent implementation of evaluations: before, during and after projects. New evaluation culture and paradigms help keep in touch with stakeholders who are not surprised by unexpected research. This approach facilitates continuous feedback and efficient management of data, information and knowledge connected with evaluated projects.

Classic evaluation paradigms should be developed toward new ones, including the progress of modern ICT technologies, AI, knowledge engineering and systems approaches. The latter item is often associated with technical issues, but it also has a wider significance in terms of planning, management, applying mathematical and scientific principles to achieve practical goals, for example, in the management and evaluation of projects.

5.3   Systems Approaches in Project Management and Evaluation

In general, there is a need for collaboration, interaction and integration at different levels (personal, projects, programs, organizational, regional and global), which leads to the creation of systems by combining different parts and objects. Integrated systems, complex systems and systems within systems (component subsystems) are built, which require specialization in different fields or interdisciplinary approaches. Individuals, interacting only with each other, subsystems or some objects (either man-made or natural) provide worse results than the whole system that is built up from these. For example, the integration of knowledge workers in combined interdisciplinary project teams creates a collaborative environment and can also ensure greater effectiveness and efficiency of actions, in comparison to the independent functioning of individual persons.

Many system definitions have been formulated, and one of these in particular treats the system as a collection of functions or activities working together within an organization and serving achieving its goals (Evans 2011). System (holistic) thinking is the approach of dealing with interdependent sets of variables complementary to analytical thinking, while analytical thinking is the approach of handling with independent sets of variables (Gharajedaghi 2011).

The use of systems approaches allows the taking into account of the multiple aspects and uncertainties of analyzed projects. The usefulness of these approaches results from the ever-growing complexity of the structure and interdependence of the objects related to socio-economic projects. Complex projects in the form of systems with a complex structure consist of multiple objects that are interconnected. There are also specific relationships with the turbulent environment, which are mostly uncertain and ambiguous. The applied systems approaches can be used not only during the building of a particular evaluation model, but also during its further improvement. The process of improvement demands a sequence of the following objects: function, structure and process in a given context (Gharajedaghi 2011).

In addition to the term 'systems approach', the literature also uses related terms: systems, systems analysis, systems research, systems science, systems theory, systems paradigm, systems thinking and systems school.

In today's world, projects are often characterized by considerable complexity and multidimensional aspects, and the built systems models are merely their simplified mathematical representations. In the case of building formalized mathematical models of projects, many important and key elements are usually omitted, which affect proper planning and implementation (Boccara 2010). The use of systems approaches in evaluation processes allows going beyond the perspective of simple calculations within the optimization perspective performed on insufficiently accurate models (Turner et al. 2010).

The subject of research, conforming to systems approaches, is systems understood as a set of interrelated elements, each of which is linked directly or indirectly to a different element (Ackoff 1971). The evaluated projects can be analyzed from the point of view of systems approaches as stand-alone systems or as subsystems constituting elements of a larger whole, that is, the organizations within which they are implemented. The project systems have subsystems that form part of them, for example, the subsystems of a project team (of a formal organizational subsystem and an informal social subsystem) or subsystems of project objectives.

Using systems thinking, it can be assumed that the essence of the project is the implementation of conversion processes of specific inputs (resources) into output products, services, effects and ultimately profits (Kerzner 2009). The input-output conversion can be considered according to the cause-and-effect relationship and it has a different form for commercial and public projects. In the case of public projects, the use of input resources and project activities should result in a variety of outputs (tangible and intangible products), outcomes (higher level benefits) and impacts (top-level strategic goals).

In accordance with the systems approach, a project makes a whole that is isolated from the environment and is composed of logically structured subsystems and their elements that interact with each other and are usually interconnected. A systems approach allows for the systematic solution of problems resulting from these particular subsystems as well as the whole (Kerzner 2009). Within the framework of the systems, a series of activities is carried out in order to achieve the objectives set earlier in accordance with the goals of the organization within which the projects are implemented.

Systems can be divided into simple systems, complicated systems and complex systems. In contrast to simple systems, complicated systems are characterized by a relatively large number of components interacting with each other, while complex systems can be created by integrating systems of other types. A particular case of this kind is the system of systems, consisting of complex systems where it is not usually possible to specify the initial rules of operation and their subsequent implementation (Eisner 2005) as well as the emergent rules that should be used in such a case (Nunes Amaral and Uzzi 2007). Rules formation (emergence), taking into account the dynamics of complex changes in particular elements (subsystems) may take place, for example, in the process of systems learning. This is applicable to the identification and analysis of such systems as, for instance, marketing research into individual and collective opinions, behaviors and attitudes, socio-economic policy systems, and systems of economic views theoretically justifying various policies and others (Roychoudhuri 2010).

The application of systems approaches makes it possible to build holistic and comprehensive models of evaluated projects. Thanks to the synergy effect, the integration of many objects is more advantageous, when compared to a simple sum of the performance of each individual object. Systems approaches ensure the possibility of taking into account the interdisciplinarity of objectives and tasks of the built systems as well as the qualitative and difficult to measure features of project evaluation criteria. Qualitative evaluation criteria often play a more important role than quantitative factors. Moreover, it is a characteristic feature of any research carried out in management sciences, which to a large extent pertains to human behaviors—which cannot be easily interpreted.

Taking into account the multidimensionality and multidisciplinarity of research related to project evaluation is made possible by treating the evaluation process as a system, and modeling using systems approaches, systems science and systems theories (e.g. General Systems Theory (Bertalanffy L. von. 1973), Complex-Adaptive Systems, Chaos Theory), Integral Theory, business and management sciences and new technologies in computer science (e.g. AI and Knowledge Engineering).

In accordance with the interdisciplinary concept of systems science, selected system sciences (economics, management, praxeology, computer science, cybernetics) can be used together with basic systems science— general systems theory, which is useful in conducting general-methodological deliberations. It is possible to integrate the following sciences within one system: economics (concerns the study of economic systems), management theory (related to organizational systems), praxeology (mainly objectives and systems efficiency), and computer science related to cybernetics (control and information processing systems). In the process of modeling complex project management and evaluation systems, methodological concepts based on the synthesis (integration) of these system sciences can be used.

One of the first manifestations of system sciences integration was the appointment (by representatives of various disciplines) of the scientific organization Society for General Systems Theory, transformed later into the International Society for Systems Science (Skyttner 2001). Among the founders were, among others, biologist L. von Bertalanffy and economist K. Boulding, who was one of the first to publish works on the need to search for applications of General Systems Theory in economics and management (Boulding 1956).

In accordance with the idea of systems sciences integration, methods and systems coming from different areas, fields and disciplines of science, for example, sociology, economics, management and operations research (in particular as related to solving multi-criteria problems) can be used jointly in a single evaluation system. Systems approaches are also practical and easy to apply when it is also necessary to solve real problems with the use of modern information technologies. Such approaches also allow for simplified models of complex phenomena and processes, as well as minimizing the negative effects of uncertainty associated with solving computationally complex problems and decision-making under uncertainty.

Modeling based on the concept of a system and its analysis is usually performed with the use of strict mathematical methods and computer computational technologies. Specific computational technologies are needed to provide the opportunity for effective systems analysis of complex, multifaceted and interdisciplinary socio-economic research challenges in today's rapidly changing and uncertain world. Such multifaceted problems requiring specific systems approaches include project management and evaluation.

Due to the considerable complexity of many projects subject to evaluation, it is worth looking for solutions enabling the modeling of evaluation processes within the framework of more general science modeling theory, which can be used in processes of evaluation model building and in the narrow fields of complex science and complexity theory. In addition to the latter, holistic thinking, systems theory, soft systems theory and other systems approaches are also important in project management and evaluation (Patton 2015). For years, systems approaches have been present in different aspects of research in the field of management sciences. For example, information and knowledge management systems, quality management systems, work environment management systems, occupational safety and health management systems, risk management systems and enterprise social responsibility systems are known. Project management methodologies were shaped to a large extent during the then dominant role of Quantitative and System School of Management Thought.

Quantitative systems approaches can be used to examine financial and economic efficiency in the process of making decisions within project management and evaluation. Then, this efficiency is determined using mathematical models implemented with the use of computer programs that operate according to algorithms developed deterministically. A number of quantitative mathematical and statistical models in the field of econometrics have been developed, which are useful in the process of making decisions concerning the evaluation of various types of projects.

Quantitative systems approaches, classical operations research based on hard systems thinking and mathematical quantitative models are useful in project evaluation processes only to a limited extent, for analysis and support of the solution of purely structured decision-making problems. Research based on quantitative mathematical models provides only a simplified picture of evaluated projects and the reality involved. In the process of building these models the following actions are usually carried out: formulation of the problem, goal and research assumptions, selection of appropriate approaches, and construction of the model and its implementation in addition to obtaining decision recommendations for its use. For computer analyses and computational calculations, the researcher selects the compounds considered by him or her to be the most important for the problem being solved. The model is related to objective function, independent variables and constraints. Objective function optimization lies in minimizing, maximizing or striving for the desired value. The obtained results may give some indication of the right decision, but the actual circumstances usually differ significantly from the simplified mathematical model.

Systems analysis, which is derived from cybernetics and operations research, is the genesis of a modern view on project planning and implementation. It also sets out an important paradigm indicating a rational model for dealing with complex and interdisciplinary problems related to the evaluation systems of contemporary projects. Precise and accurate data are relatively rarely available for these types of systems. The analyses used in project evaluation usually pertain to not only hard problems but also so-called soft issues, for example, social, environmental issues and so on. In addition, it is stressed that the complexity, multifacetedness and uncertainty of project results are constantly increasing (Williams 2002).

Hard solutions based on traditional, quantitative methods have an increasingly smaller range of applications (Turner et al. 2010). Meanwhile, in the scientific literature most of the solutions available to problems of project evaluation concerning quantitative methods and mathematical models are related to so-called hard approaches of deterministic character. Once the problem, goal and research objectives have been formulated and appropriate approaches have been chosen, models are presented to provide repeatable solutions to relatively simple problems, in line with the previously agreed objectives.

Hard systems methodologies are not suitable for cases of soft situations, complex evaluation issues and unstructured problematic situations. The use of soft systems methodologies allows the elimination of the basic limitations of hard methodologies, which do not allow the taking into account of the multidimensionality of the evaluation process and the existence of many qualitative (unstructured) factors related to, for example, stakeholders and the social and environmental aspects of evaluated projects. Integrated approaches to combined soft systems modeling and hard systems modeling are becoming increasingly important.

In a situation of dynamic development of technologies in computer science, the intuition of experts evaluating projects cannot be the only basis for decision-making processes. An important role is played by computer tools, methods and systems supporting experts in decision-making processes for evaluation; so systems based on different methods and systems of AI, for example, fuzzy sets, rough sets, knowledge-based systems, artificial neural networks and so on can complement the intellectual abilities of experts.

In the past, mainly simplified analytical mathematical methods were available. Along with the development of computer systems, numerical procedures have been improved. Systems approaches research has been contributing to the development of science and information technology for years, and current systems research is geared toward the use of advanced computing technologies to manage data, information and knowledge within a turbulent environment and uncertainty.

The application of systems approaches to project evaluation enables the building of models of interdisciplinary systems used to process and interpret various quantitative and qualitative data. The variety of data results from people often recording data imprecisely and subjectively. Data used in the evaluation process may be stored in a numerical, binary, logical and multimedia form. They can be vectors, tables, numbers which are the individual elements of vectors or tables, sequences of selected elements and so on.

The necessary and possible development of the field of project evaluation should be carried out by using consistent systems approaches, constantly verified, enriched and improved, and various methods and systems, also allowing an increase in the accuracy of the decisions made in conditions of uncertainty. High hopes can be associated with multimethodologies relying on mixing together hard and soft methodologies toward the development of mixed (integrated) systems for project evaluation. Taking into account the multidimensionality and interdisciplinarity of evaluation research is possible thanks to the application, on the basis of business and management sciences, not only of modern AI and Knowledge Engineering technologies, but also of selected system theories, such as Integral Theory.

5.4   Integral Theory and Evaluation Systems

Mixed (integrated) systems for project evaluation can be, inter alia, based on Integral Theory and related to the Integral Methodological Pluralism and All Quadrants, All Levels (AQAL) models, with eight indigenous perspectives. Integral Theory inspires the development of an ever-growing array of management instruments, methods and tools, as well as enabling evaluation studies to be carried out within individual scientific fields, thus solving cross-disciplinary research problems.

Integral Theory is still gaining in popularity and has found numerous applications in various scientific disciplines (Forman and Esbjörn-Hargens 2010). This theory is useful in the process of building mixed (integrated) systems, enabling quantitative and qualitative analyses to be conducted in social sciences research (Black 2008, Martin 2008). The AQAL model, which enables comprehensive or integral map building, covers many dimensions and levels of reality and is built from the following five types of fundamental concepts:

1. four quadrants (describing the basic dimensions of experience in four perspectives: the inside, the outside, the individual and the collective),
2. levels of existence,
3. lines (multiple intelligences development),
4. states of consciousness,
5. types (e.g. gender, personality, abilities) (Wilber 2007a).

The combined application of a systems approach and Integral Theory enables the modeling of truly holistic and comprehensive project evaluation systems.

The development of the evaluation field is characterized by a multitude of methodological trends and scientific theories. Therefore, it is useful to use a consistent Integral Theory that enables the integration of many of these trends into a systems approach in project management and evaluation. Thanks to the application of this theory, in addition to dynamically developing quantitative trends, different methodological trends can be applied concerning difficult to measure qualitative characteristics of projects. This is important because supporting decisions related to the evaluation of complex and unique projects requires the taking into account of interdisciplinary, integrated and aggregated approaches that capture their multidimensionality and multiple perspectives.

Eight indigenous perspectives allow the building of a multifaceted and multiprospect (both internal and external) picture of evaluated phenomena in four quadrants. Individual perspectives can be assigned to sets of quantitative and qualitative research methods, ensuring an integral methodological pluralism (Wilber 2007b). The form of the AQAL model, which allows for the implementation of integral methodological pluralism, as well as being a model which is useful for organizing sets of methods and systems, is shown in Fig. 5.1.

The contemporary field of project management and evaluation within business and management sciences requires holistic modeling and decision-making support, compatible with many dimensions and perspectives: economic, social, environmental, technological, ethical and others. It is often difficult to define and perform a reliable evaluation of the hierarchical structure of interdisciplinary objectives and the results achieved by the organization and its projects, which are intended to meet the needs of stakeholders. The results of integrated quantitative and qualitative analyses

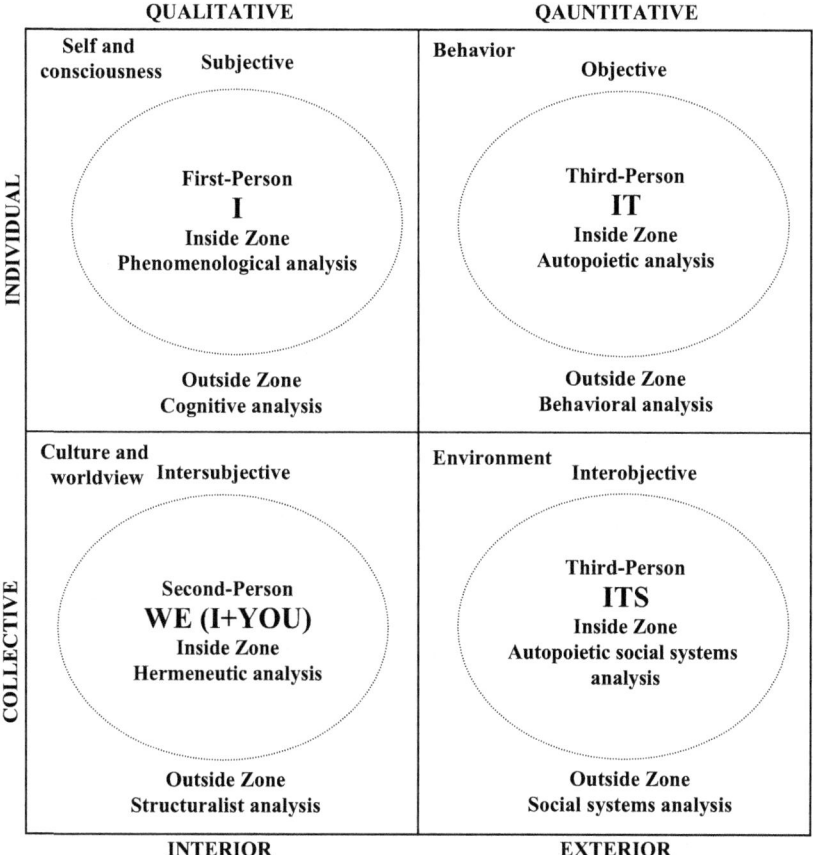

QUALITATIVE   **QAUNTITATIVE**

INDIVIDUAL

Self and
consciousness   Subjective

First-Person
I
Inside Zone
Phenomenological analysis

Outside Zone
Cognitive analysis

Behavior
Objective

Third-Person
IT
Inside Zone
Autopoietic analysis

Outside Zone
Behavioral analysis

COLLECTIVE

Culture and
worldview   Intersubjective

Second-Person
WE (I+YOU)
Inside Zone
Hermeneutic analysis

Outside Zone
Structuralist analysis

Environment   Interobjective

Third-Person
ITS
Inside Zone
Autopoietic social systems
analysis

Outside Zone
Social systems analysis

INTERIOR   **EXTERIOR**

Fig. 5.1 AQAL model. (Source: Based on Wilber (2007b), Kleineberg (2016))

are usually ambiguous, since many qualitative and poorly structured management problems cannot be quantified properly.

Moving away from the traditional quantitative project management and evaluation models toward new system models allows for the incorporation of important qualitative phenomena and their social and environmental characters. The combined use of AQAL quadrants along with management theories and paradigms allows the building of truly holistic management models, taking into consideration complex and interdisciplinary aspects based on comprehensive study of described reality.

Integral theory enables the building of holistic understanding, multi-disciplinary and complex management and project evaluation fields using many perspectives, methodologies and a meta-paradigm approach in a single coherent vision. Using this theory, it is possible to classify key schools of management thought by building a meta-theoretical epistemological framework (Fig. 5.2).

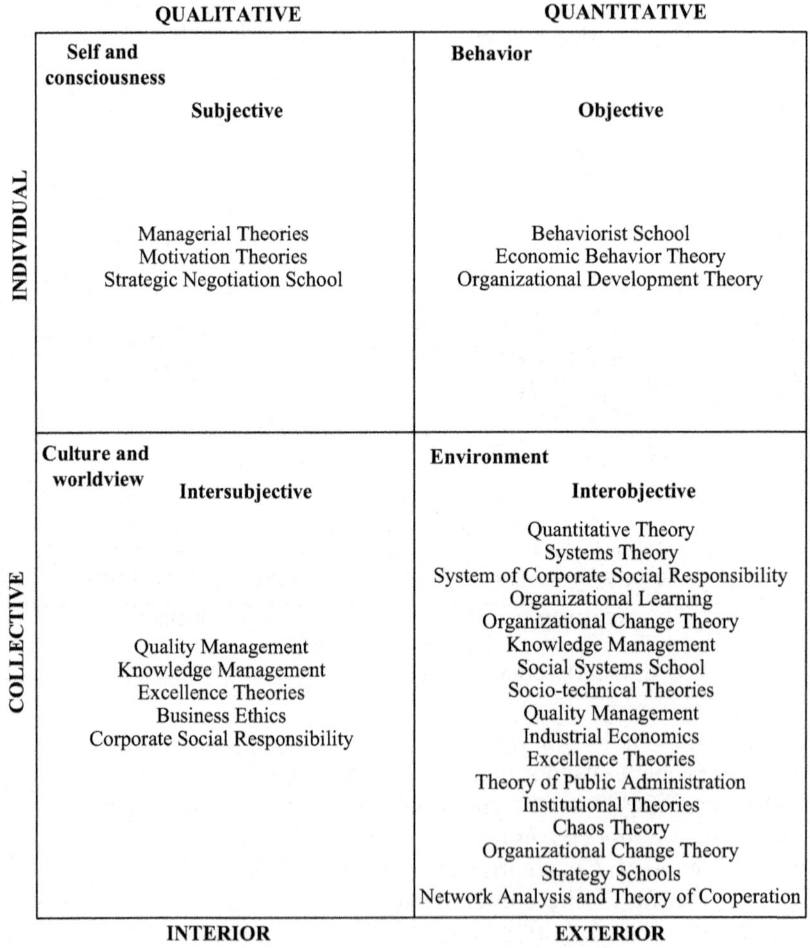

	QUALITATIVE	QUANTITATIVE
INDIVIDUAL	**Self and consciousness** Subjective Managerial Theories Motivation Theories Strategic Negotiation School	**Behavior** Objective Behaviorist School Economic Behavior Theory Organizational Development Theory
COLLECTIVE	**Culture and worldview** Intersubjective Quality Management Knowledge Management Excellence Theories Business Ethics Corporate Social Responsibility	**Environment** Interobjective Quantitative Theory Systems Theory System of Corporate Social Responsibility Organizational Learning Organizational Change Theory Knowledge Management Social Systems School Socio-technical Theories Quality Management Industrial Economics Excellence Theories Theory of Public Administration Institutional Theories Chaos Theory Organizational Change Theory Strategy Schools Network Analysis and Theory of Cooperation
	INTERIOR	EXTERIOR

Fig. 5.2 AQAL quadrants, management theories and paradigms. (Source: Based on Robledo (2014))

Attention should be drawn to the classic praxeology (theory of human action) located in the upper-left quadrant, which concerns individual human actions according to methodological individualism (Murphy 2008)—Fig. 5.3. Praxeological terminology concerning various types of evaluation is useful in the implementation of processes of building general models of project evaluation systems, which might form the basis for constructing further, more formalized descriptions of the examined fragment of reality. Various trends of praxeology are inspiring within the study of project management theory and evaluation.

Because organizations and projects are based on collective activities, the lower quadrants (especially the lower-right quadrant, e.g. related to systems and social sciences) are essential (Robledo 2014). Project management and evaluation should also be assigned to the lower quadrants, in connection with their collective character. In particular, these areas should be linked to the lower-right quadrant, in line with a systemic view of projects and evaluation processes. The lower-left quadrant contains qualitative evaluation and soft systems methodology. For the lower-right quadrant, quantitative evaluation and hard systems methodology are assigned.

	QUALITATIVE	QUANTITATIVE
INDIVIDUAL	**Subjective** Project Manager Motivation Praxeology	**Objective** Evaluation Based on Measurable Indicator Monitoring Indicators
COLLECTIVE	**Intersubjective** Project Management and Evaluation Qualitative Evaluation Soft Evaluation Systems Project Quality Management Project Knowledge Management	**Interobjective** Project Management Systems Evaluation Systems Quantitative Evaluation Systems Theory Hard Evaluation Systems Project Knowledge Management System Sustainability in Project Management
	INTERIOR	**EXTERIOR**

Fig. 5.3   AQAL quadrants and evaluation systems

To solve a complicated problem of building a model of a comprehensive projects evaluation system, one should search using quantitative-qualitative systems approaches and integral theory to project evaluation, in addition to new and innovative approaches to evaluation based on concepts from computational intelligence methods. Research concerning the theory and applications of mixed methods and mixed systems in business and management sciences has not been well represented so far.

5.5   Mixed Systems Studies Introduction

The explanation presented in the previous sections on systems approaches and Integral Theory provides a basis for the presentation of mixed systems studies, understood as integration of hard and soft problem-solving methodologies in systems science. These systemic methodologies differ fundamentally, and their combination has the potential to provide many new opportunities, but sometimes also poses a significant challenge.

Hard systems methodology involves advanced analytical quantitative methods, deterministic complexity, operations research (the sub-field of the mathematics branch called applied mathematics), structured decision-making methods, decision science, interdisciplinary management science and systems analysis. The scientific approaches and methods used in this methodology are generally used to solve well-defined problems for which one can find single, optimum solutions. This methodology is related to searching for connections, comparisons and causal relationships between variables by using mathematical, statistical and numerical computational techniques.

The soft systems methodology is different and concerns solving problems that are closer to assessed reality; it does not assume the existence of a quantitatively measurable objective reality, which is poorly defined and of a qualitative nature. For these kinds of problems, it is important to consider human factors and different project stakeholders' points of view, to seek a better understanding of the problems assessed, rather than just looking for the right quantitative solutions in order to be optimal. Solutions are related to non-measurable complex problems which are unpredictable in nature, non-repeatable and non-deterministic.

It is advisable to combine hard and soft systems methodologies and the use of quantitative-qualitative systems approaches. Systems approaches are practical and easy to use in solving complex problems using modern information technologies. In accordance with the concept of mixed systems studies, the integration of often different methodologies, methods and systems from various areas and disciplines can be applied together within the individual comprehensive evaluation systems of complex projects.

Mixed Methods Studies (multimethod research, multimethodology, methodological pluralism) contain the use of more than one method in project evaluation processes. These studies can be undertaken considering many scientific perspectives and paradigms and they also make it possible to take into account the performance of classical and intelligent approaches to the modeling of modern project evaluation systems.

Mixed (integrated) systems involve the integration of both quantitative and qualitative systems in project evaluation processes. The principles of selecting methods for these systems can provide specific and useful skills and make the integration process easier. They are useful in making decisions about identifying which approaches, methods and systems would be best for a particular model of mixed systems.

Bibliometric studies show that in the scientific literature on data basic features characterization associated with the conducted studies, quantitative approaches are predominant (approx. 70%). They are mainly based on percentages, frequency counts and descriptive statistics. The same research shows that qualitative approaches constitute approximately 22% and mixed methods designs are the least frequently used (approximately 9%) (Togia and Malliari 2017). Therefore, there is a research gap and a shortage of literature on studies about mixed methods and systems designs and their application.

Mixed research is not easy to implement and requires considerable knowledge and experience from evaluators in the field of using quantitative evaluation systems as well as qualitative systems. Increasing their popularity is desirable and possible if available publications and educated experts in the field, as well as the number of studies carried out in accordance with methodological pluralism grows.

The advantages of mixed research, among other aspects, include (Johnson and Onwuegbuzie 2004):

- potential opportunities resulting from combined reliance on the advantages of different quantitative and qualitative systems,
- the use of two different systems reduces the weaknesses of one system through the advantages of the other,
- the use of more methods and systems in research makes it possible to increase the reliability of the results and the conclusions to be drawn,

- qualitative description can enrich quantitative research results and qualitative descriptions can be further refined by precise numerical results,
- there are potential opportunities to extend the scope of research to problems that could not be solved by individual research methods and qualitative or quantitative systems,
- the use of multiple methods and systems of a different nature can provide more knowledge useful for developing the theory and practice of research,
- a larger number of research methods and systems provide a stronger basis for the higher generalization of the achieved results.

Taking into account the multifaceted and multidisciplinary nature of project evaluation, research is made possible by treating the evaluation process as a system and modeling using the integration of hard and soft methodologies, systems approaches, Integral Theory, business and management sciences and new technologies based on AI and knowledge engineering. The necessary and possible development of the field of project evaluation should be made by continuous verification and enrichment of the degree of differentiation of methods and systems and their improvement, in order to increase the degree of accuracy of decisions taken. Application of AI and knowledge engineering systems in integrated systems justifies the use of the term 'mixed intelligent systems'.

REFERENCES

Ackoff, R. (1971, July). Towards a System of Systems Concepts. *Management Science, 17*(11), 661–671.

Astbury, B. & Leeuw, F. L. (2010). Unpacking Black Boxes: Mechanisms and Theory Building in Evaluation. *American Journal of Evaluation 31*(3), 363–381.

Bachtler, J., & Wren, C. (2006, April). Evaluation of European Union Cohesion Policy. Research Questions and Policy Challenges. *Regional Studies, 40*(2), 143–153.

Bertalanffy, L. von (1973). *General System Theory: Foundations, Development, Applications.* New York: G. Braziller.

Black, T. G. (2008). Applying AQAL to the Quantitative/Qualitative Debate in Social Sciences Research. *Journal of Integral Theory and Practice, 3*(1), 1–15.

Boccara, N. (2010). *Modeling Complex Systems.* New York/Dordrecht/Heidelberg/London: Springer.

Boulding, K. (1956). General System Theory: The Skeleton of Science. *Management of Science.*

Drucker, P. F. (2001). *Management Challenges for the 21st Century.* New York: Harper Business.

Eisner, H. (2005). *Managing Complex Systems. Thinking Outside the Box.* New Jersey: Wiley-Interscience.

Evans, J. R. (2011). *Quality & Performance Excellence.* Mason: South-Western Cengage Learning.

Forman, M. D., & Esbjörn-Hargens, S. (2010). The Academic Emergence of Integral Theory. Reflections On and Clarifications of the 1st Biennial Integral Theory Conference. In S. Esbjörn-Hargens (Ed.), *Integral theory in action: Applied, theoretical, and constructive perspectives on the AQAL model.* New York: SUNY Press.

Gharajedaghi, J. (2011). *Systems Thinking. Managing Chaos and Complexity: A Platform for Designing Business Architecture.* Burlington: Morgan Kaufmann, Elsevier.

Goldkuhl, G. (2012, March). Pragmatism vs Interpretivism in Qualitative Information Systems Research. *European Journal of Information Systems, 21*(2), 135–146.

Johnson, R. B., & Onwuegbuzie, A. J. (2004, October). Mixed Methods Research: A Research Paradigm Whose Time Has Come. *Educational Researcher, 33*(7), 14–26.

Kerzner, H. (2009). *Project Management: A Systems Approach to Planning, Scheduling, and Controlling.* New Jersey: John Wiley & Sons.

Kleineberg, M. (2016). *Integral Methodological Pluralism: An Organizing Principle for Method Classification.* Conference: 14th International ISKO Conference. Knowledge Organization in a Sustainable World.

Martin, J. A. (2008). Integral Research as a Practical Mixed-Methods Framework: Clarifying the Role of Integral Methodological Pluralism. *Journal of Integral Theory and Practice, 3,* 155–164.

Mertens, D. M., & Wilson, A. T. (2012). *Program Evaluation Theory and Practice: A Comprehensive Guide.* New York: The Guilford Press.

Murphy, R. P. (2008). *Study Guide to Human Action: A Treatise on Economics.* Auburn, Alabama: Ludwig von Mises Institute.

Nunes Amaral, L. A., & Uzzi, B. (2007). Complex Systems. A New Paradigm for the Integrative Study of Management, Physical and Technological Systems. *Management Science, 53*(7):1033–1035.

Olsson, N. O. E., & Bull-Berg, H. (2015). Use of Big Data in Project Evaluations. *International Journal of Managing Projects in Business, 8*(3), 491–512.

Patton, M. Q. (1975). *Alternative evaluation research paradigm.* Grand Forks: North Dakota Study Group on Evaluation, University of North Dakota.

Patton, M. Q. (1987). *Creative Evaluation.* California: SAGE Publications Inc. Thousand Oaks California 91320.

Patton, M. Q. (2011). *Essentials of Utilization-Focused Evaluation*. SAGE Publications Inc. Thousand Oaks California 91320.

Patton, M. Q. (2015). *Qualitative Research & Evaluation Methods. Integrating Theory and Practice*. Thousand Oaks/London/New Delhi: SAGE Publications Inc.

Pawson, R., & Tilley, N. (2004). *Realist Evaluation*. London: Sage Publications Ltd.

Picciotto, R. (1999). Towards an Economics of Evaluation. *Evaluation, 5*(1), 7–22.

Robledo, M. A. (2014). Building an Integral Metatheory of Management. *European Management Journal, 32*, 535–546.

Roychoudhuri, C. (2010). The Consilient Epistemology: Structuring Evolution of Our Logical Thinking. In C. Rangacharyulu, E. Haven (Eds.), *Proceedings of the First Interdisciplinary Chess Interactions Conference*.

Royse, D., Thyer, B. A., & Padgett, D. K. (2010). *Program Evaluation. An Introduction*. Wadsworth: Cengage Learning.

Saunders, M. N. K., Thornhill, A., & Lewis, P. (2007). *Research Methods for Business Students*. Pearson.

Skyttner, L. (2001). *General Systems Theory: Ideas & Applications*. Singapore: World Scientific Pub Co Inc.

Tavistock Institute. (2003). *The Evaluation of Socio-Economic Development: The Guide*. London: Tavistock Institute in association with GHK, IRS.

Togia, A., & Malliari, A. (2017). Research Methods in Library and Information Science, Qualitative Versus Quantitative Research. In S. Oflazoglu (Ed.), *Qualitative Versus Quantitative Research*. Rijeka, Croatia: InTech.

Turner, R. J., Huemann, M., Anbari, F. T., & Bredillet, C. N. (2010). *Perspectives on Projects*. Abingdon: Routledge.

Wilber, K. (2007a). *Integral Spirituality: A Startling New Role for Religion in the Modern and Postmodern World*. Boston/London: Integral Books.

Wilber, K. (2007b). *The Integral Vision: A Very Short Introduction to the Revolutionary Integral Approach to Life, God, the Universe, and Everything*. Boston & London: Shambhala.

Williams, T. (2002). *Modelling Complex Projects*. Chichester: John Wiley and Sons.

CHAPTER 6

Modeling Mixed Intelligent Systems

Abstract Modeling mixed intelligent systems constitute a summary of research regarding building their models and designs. The author proposes a Multi-Level Evaluation Model, Integral Multi-Level Evaluation Model and an example of design of a mixed intelligent system for comprehensive project evaluation. Multi-Level Evaluation Models have several evaluation dimensions and four levels of project management and evaluation: projects, programs, project and program portfolios, as well as the organizational strategic level. The second model is an example of Integral Theory application that constitutes a kind of 'meta-paradigm' that allows for the combination of separate paradigms, approaches and systems into an interrelated framework for multifaceted project evaluation. An example of the design of a mixed intelligent system for comprehensive project evaluation is based on convergent parallel mixed systems and hybrid mixed systems. This mixed intelligent system uses the parallel application of two intelligent systems: a rule-based system and neural networks. The end of the chapter concerns historical reference to evaluation systems development, as well as a feasible vision for conducting this research in the future.

Keywords Mixed intelligent systems • Integral Multi-Level Evaluation Model • Mixed methods research designs • Evaluation systems development

© The Author(s) 2018   91
T. A. Grzeszczyk, *Mixed Intelligent Systems*,
https://doi.org/10.1007/978-3-319-91158-8_6

6.1   RESEARCH QUESTIONS

Specifying research questions is a fundamental step in research concerning modeling mixed (integrated) methods and systems. As a result of taking up the search for answers to these questions, the opening up of a vast research space is observed. In the context of searching new comprehensive evaluation models, the research conducted within this space seems to be promising.

The research questions should be adapted to the research problem posed by the existence of a certain knowledge gap. Research carried out in connection with the pursuit of the agreed research objective and the search for answers to the research questions should lead to a solution for the research problem. The way these questions are formulated in the beginning determines the subsequent application of quantitative, qualitative or mixed research methodologies, methods and systems. Studies based on the questions asked should be feasible.

Generally, research questions for different research perspectives and methodologies have different characters and may be stated as:

1. quantitative research questions (related to deductive searching for connections, comparisons, causal relationships between variables),
2. qualitative research questions (concerning inductive exploring, describing and depth of understanding of phenomena which are difficult to precisely and quantitatively measure),
3. a set of both types of question related to mixed research.

Adapting research questions to a specific research problem is initially a matter of defining its quantitative, qualitative or mixed character. Quantitative research questions can have the following forms:

- descriptive—allowing the quantification of variables, the number of factors and so on,
- causal (relationship-based)—associations, causal relationships, quantitative trends, correlation and interaction between variables,
- predictive—forecasting the value of the selected variable,
- comparative—comparing the values of variables.

Qualitative research questions regarding discovering, exploring, describing and understanding phenomena which cannot be accurately quantified will not be determined by causal relationships and so on. Qualitative questions are more general in nature than quantitative questions. Therefore, it is worth making sure that systems of qualitative questions are built, in order to provide more detailed, structured and targeted research based on these questions. So, for particular research problems it is useful to formulate brief and open-ended main questions, along with several corresponding sub-questions.

Questions related to mixed research should be adapted, as follows, to the specificities of this type of research (Creswell and Plano Clark 2010):

- it is worth separating quantitative, qualitative and mixed research questions from each other in order to facilitate their proper formulation, and then carrying out research based on these,
- forms of mixed research questions depend on the chosen type of study design,
- questions may concern a more general level or a more specific level of study design (Creswell and Plano Clark suggest a more specific level).

The division into three types of research questions presented in this section is not well established in scientific literature. There is often an opinion about the need to use only quantitative and qualitative questions, and that the definition of questions related to mixed research is not appropriate.

6.2   Model Assumptions

The processes of entering and processing data, information and knowledge in the built models of mixed intelligent systems should be implemented in a way that ensures their practical usefulness and universality, which is expressed in the possibilities of evaluating different types of projects. Thus, the following basic research assumptions were adopted.

1. Models are based on a mixed intelligent systems concept that allows the simultaneous use of both selected intelligent and classical evaluation methods and systems combination.
2. Both symbolic as well as non-symbolic intelligent systems can be used in the model.
3. Researches should be carried out systemically, multidisciplinarily, comprehensively and with many evaluation aspects.
4. Models are universal evaluation tools, characterized by their versatility, capable of comprehensive evaluation of various projects and taking criteria desirable by the system user into consideration.
5. The universality of the model is also expressed in the possibilities of being used in various types of evaluation, for example, formative and summative.

6. Evaluation processes are treated as systems and they are modeled by using the integration of hard and soft methodologies, systems approaches, Integral Theory and new technologies based on AI and Knowledge Engineering.
7. A truly holistic way of thinking is used, which is compatible with many evaluation dimensions and perspectives: economic, social, environmental, technological, ethical and so on.
8. Systems should be equipped with a feedback control loop and include changes that occur in complex dynamic systems of evaluation.
9. Model flexibility should be apparent in the possibility of the relative ease of introducing changes to evaluation methods and systems used, as well as by using different kinds of data—quantitative and qualitative.
10. The model enables easy changes to the methods and systems used and ensures large scalability.
11. Correct model functioning in the case of the occurrence of uncertain, incomplete and inconsistent input of empirical data should be ensured.

Using the concept of mixed intelligent systems enables the simultaneous use of selected intelligent as well as classic evaluation methods and systems. From the previous considerations regarding design and selection of mixed intelligent systems, the features of various possible solutions arise. Most of the available designs are characterized by flexibility, which relies on the relative ease of introducing changes to the applied methods and evaluation systems. The individual subsystems that create the whole mixed evaluation system may have a fundamentally different nature of operation and ways of processing various types of quantitative and qualitative data.

In addition to ensuring easy modifications to mixed intelligent systems, it is not difficult to ensure good scalability and expand such systems. In the process of expanding mixed intelligent systems, one can take into consideration not only various types of quantitative and qualitative systems, but also systems operating in accordance with different types of knowledge representation: symbolic and non-symbolic.

According to the systems approach, subsystems that are elements of mixed intelligent systems can also be systems created as a result of integration (hybridization) of methods and systems. The modification and development of mixed intelligent systems may involve the introduction of further solutions characteristic of both hard and soft system methodologies, deterministic and non-deterministic solutions and various types of AI based systems and knowledge engineering technologies.

The evaluation processes should be implemented systematically, multidisciplinarily, comprehensively and taking into account many aspects of evaluation. The application of integral theory enables the building of holistic and multidisciplinary understanding of complex project evaluation using many perspectives, methodologies and a meta-paradigm approach in a single coherent vision. In such a truly holistic way of thinking about project evaluation, it is possible to ensure compliance with many dimensions and perspectives: economic, social, environmental, technological, ethical and others. It is possible to provide analysis at various levels (operational, tactical and strategic) taking into consideration individual projects, programs and portfolios.

Mixed intelligent systems are universal and capable of the comprehensive evaluation of various projects in accordance with the criteria resulting from program documents systems (for public projects), internal requirements applicable to various non-commercial and commercial organizations, and also other special criteria formulated by the system users. The universality of mixed intelligent systems is also expressed in the possibilities of using its various types of evaluation: ex-ante, ex-post and ongoing. They are also useful in the case of formative and summative evaluation.

According to the adopted systems approach, mixed intelligent systems should be equipped with a feedback loop and take into account changes taking place in complex dynamic evaluation systems and within their turbulent environment. The use of intelligent systems and AI methods also allows the correct functioning of the model in the case of uncertain, incomplete and inconsistent empirical data used to build the evaluation knowledge bases.

6.3   BUILDING INTEGRAL MULTI-LEVEL EVALUATION MODEL

The reflections on the Multi-Level Evaluation Model presented below are important for developing evaluation studies based on systems approaches. In the modeling process, one aims at obtaining a model of a comprehensive projects evaluation system which is a simplified reflection of a part of reality based on the system approach.

The application of multidisciplinary systems approaches allows all-in application of different research methods and systems, qualitative and quantitative analyses and takes many factors, that is, economic, social, cultural, political and technological into account. Emphasizing social and environmental aspects basically distinguishes a comprehensive project evaluation system from field and fragmentary evaluation systems used, for example, with reference to commercial, investment and other projects. In these cases, the most important are quantitative financial and economic aspects.

Application of systems approaches also enables integration of different conceptions and methodological soft and hard approaches along with the use of new ICT technologies in the process of building a model of a comprehensive project evaluation system. In particular, using ICT technology based on a system of soft computing methods is important. They belong to the currently dynamically developing field of science research defined as Computational Intelligence (CI). This deals with the machinery implementation of heuristic algorithms, inspired biologically and mathematically. A similar term is Artificial Intelligence (AI).

Important comprehensive evaluation methods result from the CI and AI fields. Approaches of this kind are defined as 'intelligent'. They enable the obtaining of formal representation of qualitative granular information about evaluated projects, in the form of granules of information. Intelligent systems have an ability to learn so-called absorption and generalization of knowledge gained. Thanks to their help, reasoning and thinking mechanisms can be created. Project evaluation systems based on CI and AI accept empirical data characterized by uncertainty, inaccuracy, logical inconsistency and incompleteness. Algorithms used in such systems do not always find precise mathematical justification for their correctness. Inspirations for their elaboration are often intuitive or observed in a natural environment surrounding a person.

The application of a multidisciplinary systems approach and new ICT technologies, particularly those based on CI and AI systems, provides the opportunity to develop a model of a comprehensive project evaluation system. Ignoring these methods makes it impossible to create a complete system of methods for comprehensive project evaluation and to reach the maturity stage of the project evaluation process.

The design of the project evaluation model should take into account the management and evaluation carried out at many levels of the organization, as well as various factors and dimensions, for example, social, economic, environmental, technological, ethical and so on. Evaluation of projects, programs and project portfolios requires taking into consideration many aspects, not only directly but also indirectly related to implementation. In particular, this applies to the management and evaluation processes of highly complex projects, requiring significant resources to be devoted to their implementation, causing significant impacts and sometimes even permanent and irreversible social changes, also occurring in the natural environment. Therefore, multi-level holistic evaluation processes should consider the effects analyzed in many dimensions connected with sustainability.

Today, the field of project management and evaluation requires holistic modeling and support for decision-making, which are compatible with many dimensions and perspectives. Within this field, which is a relatively new and distinct field within the framework of management sciences, various new research trends are being developed, considering the multidimensional nature, complexity and uniqueness of project activities. This type of research is timely and important, since more and more organizations are undertaking the planning and implementing of projects with a relatively broad scope and complexity.

The additional aspects of the evaluation modeling process are related to the fact that more and more projects are not of ordinary, commercial nature and their relatively easily measurable effects are of secondary importance. In addition, the set of stakeholders is diverse and difficult to identify and study. The hierarchical structure of interdisciplinary objectives responding to stakeholders' needs is often difficult to identify and evaluate. The results of quantitative and qualitative analyses are usually ambiguous, while their multidimensional evaluation is in itself a complex and unique project. In addition, it is not yet generally accepted that organizations should also take into account evaluation criteria related, for example, to aspects of difficult to measure, long-term, sustainable and responsible development of projects, programs and project portfolios and organizations implementing these (Grzeszczyk 2016a).

Sustainability and sustainable development are linked to the aforementioned dimensions (economic, social and environmental). In the case of research conducted within a broader perspective, one can use the experience of development economics concerning the development of low income countries. The activities of the organization, and large complex projects, programs and project portfolios can even influence the shape of socio-economic models and stimulate growth, which is aggregated at the level of many regions and countries. Within business and management sciences, sustainability is most often studied at the level of various organizations, and sometimes implemented projects.

There is an increasing role for sustainability in developing business and management theory and practice. In connection with the growing number of studies related to sustainability in project management, one can even observe the emergence of a new sustainability school of thinking in project management. The development of this school of project management is determined by societal perspectives, stakeholder approach, triple bottom line criteria (economic, social and environmental) and a values-based approach (Silvius 2017).

The importance of issues of various dimensions of sustainability, their growing importance in project management and the emerging new sustainability school of thinking in project management justify their inclusion in the process of general project evaluation modeling. Figure 6.1 shows the Multi-Level Evaluation Model with several evaluation dimensions and four levels of project management and evaluation. The lowest level applies to individual projects. The second and third level evaluations are related to programs, as well as to project and program portfolios. The last, highest level concerns evaluation at the strategic level of the organization.

Despite recognizing the importance of sustainability in a project management context, it is still under-represented in scientific publications, when compared to the literature on sustainability concerning organiza-

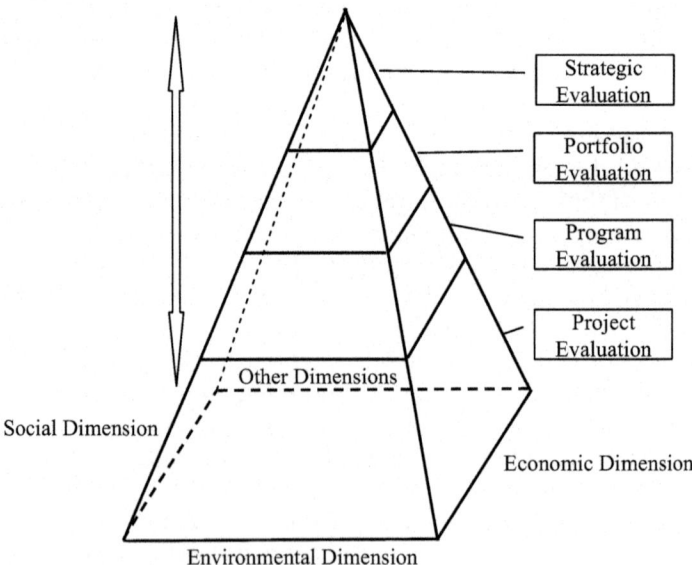

Fig. 6.1   Multi-Level Evaluation Model

tional, national, regional and global levels. As sustainability in project management and evaluation is relatively new and there is a research gap in this field, it is worth familiarizing oneself with the currently small range of literature in this field (Aarseth et al. 2017) and proposing new solutions in the field of project evaluation, taking into account sustainability.

The application of systems thinking is a good way to develop holistic, comprehensive and mixed systems of project evaluation, project sustainability-related discussion regarding different perceptions in multiple perspectives, the interconnectivity of diverse dimensions, networks of interactive relationships (connections in different contexts), project scopes and impact boundaries. Combining such extensive problems, in addition to developing new holistic models for project management and evaluation, toward mixed intelligent systems, is possible as a result of the use of integral (inclusive, comprehensive, embracing, non-marginalizing) approaches (Fig. 6.2). They constitute a kind of 'meta-paradigm' that allows the combining of separate paradigms, approaches and systems into an interrelated framework of paradigms, approaches and systems that are mutually enriching (Wilber 2003).

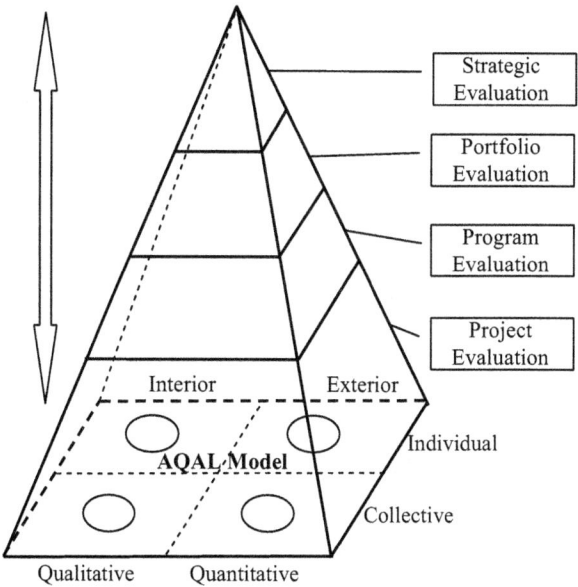

Fig. 6.2 Integral Multi-Level Evaluation Model

	QUALITATIVE	QAUNTITATIVE
INDIVIDUAL	**Subjective** Project Internal Environment Project Internal Stakeholder Project Manager Consultant Supplier Contractor Client Financier	**Objective** Measurable Evaluation Indicators Applications Human-Expert Evaluations Quantitative Expert Evaluations Social Impact Assessment Environmental Impact Assessment Economic, Cultural Impact, Hazard and Risk Assessment
COLLECTIVE	**Intersubjective** Project Internal Environment Project Internal Stakeholders Project Team Commitment Authority Steering Committee Consultants Suppliers Contractors Clients Financiers	**Interobjective** Projects External Surroundings External Stakeholder Environment Quantitative Systems Approaches Economic, Socio-cultural, Technological, Political-legal and other Systems
	INTERIOR	**EXTERIOR**

Fig. 6.3 AQAL quadrants for the first evaluation level

Figure 6.3 shows examples of AQAL quadrants for the first evaluation level of the Integral Multi-Level Evaluation Model. In order to carry out analyses in line with the systems approach, the evaluated project should be treated as a system within which internal subsystems of project implementation can be distinguished. Aspects related to project implementing organizations can also be classified as internal. Exterior aspects are related to the closer and further environments of projects.

New reflections on the Multi-Level Evaluation Model presented in this section are based on the author's earlier scientific achievements concerning comprehensive evaluation systems. Achievements and discoveries in this field are important for generalizing research results for their usefulness in the development of evaluation studies based on systems approaches. Reflections on the general model, with several evaluation dimensions and four levels of project management and evaluation, are the basis for showing such designs and mixed intelligent systems to be useful in this field.

6.4   Designs and Selection of Mixed Intelligent Systems

There are definitely many advantages resulting from the use of mixed evaluation systems. However, in research practice it turns out that these advantages are no longer relevant in the case of erroneous design and selection of mixed solutions. A wide selection of classical and intelligent systems, as well as quantitative and qualitative systems is available, and these can be combined in different ways. This section deals with the choice of the most appropriate designs for mixed intelligent systems.

Within mixed research technology the following can be distinguished: mixed methods design, mixed models design and mixed systems design. Based on a systems approach and Integral Theory, mixed intelligent systems designs can be produced with the use of traditional and intelligent systems that constitute subsystems of larger mixed systems. The particular types of mixed systems differ in terms of usefulness and applicability within processes of comprehensive project evaluation.

In the simplest case, the integration process may involve the determination of the weighted average of quantitative results obtained as a result of calculations carried out within subsystems. However, this can only concern quantitative analysis subsystems. In the case of multifaceted project evaluation, the results of the various subsystems generally have different characters—quantitative and qualitative.

There are several potentially available ways of integrating subsystems operating in accordance with different methods of evaluation. In particular, parallel coupled systems and sequential coupled systems may be considered. Also, hybrid mixed systems are possible. These systems occur when one system is used for performing the specified functions in the second system and forms its integral part, but each of these maintains its individuality. Such mixed systems are used relatively rare, because there may be difficulties with modeling processes and their implementation (Grzeszczyk 2016b).

The three following primary models now dominate within the mixed methods and systems used in social sciences (Creswell 2014):

1. convergent parallel mixed systems, used for the comprehensive study of research problems based on quantitative and qualitative forms of data, which are collected and analyzed in parallel, and then the obtained results of analyses are integrated,

2. exploratory sequential mixed systems, in which two stages are distinguished—first the implementation of preliminary qualitative research, and then the basic quantitative study,
3. explanatory sequential mixed systems, in which the initial quantitative study precedes the basic qualitative research (initial quantitative analysis results are explained additionally on the basis of qualitative analyses).

Parallel mixed systems (triangulation convergence design—Fig. 6.4) are characterized by the independent action of different subsystems. The parallel combination of subsystems can even use completely different systems and methods of analysis. The final results are achieved as an effect of the integration of results from individual subsystems.

Sequential mixed systems are characterized by the fact that the one of the subsystem's outputs is the second subsystem's input. Subsystems are connected in series (cascade) and implement the next phase of processing in further consecutive actions (Fig. 6.5).

The significant advantage of mixed systems (both sequential and parallel) is the potential for individual implementation of relatively simple subsystems. This allows easy modeling and implementation, as compared to hybrid mixed systems. Parallel mixed systems are simpler in design and application and are characterized by considerable flexibility, because there is the possibility of integrating quantitative and qualitative methods with classical and intelligent evaluation methods. For these reasons, they are

Fig. 6.4 Parallel mixed systems. (Source: Based on Creswell and Plano Clark (2010))

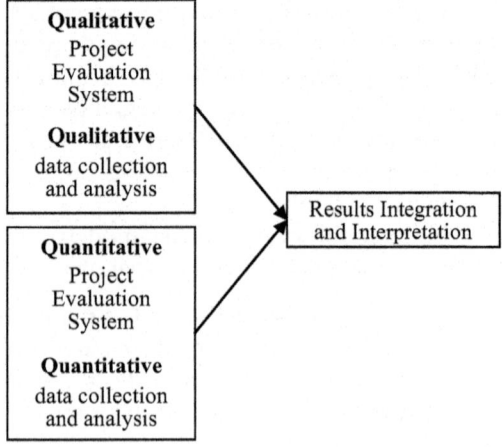

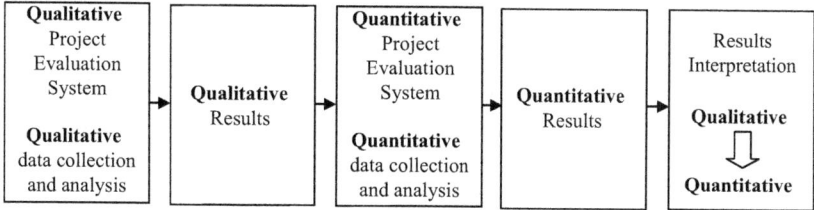

Fig. 6.5 Design of exploratory sequential mixed systems. (Source: Based on Creswell and Plano Clark (2010))

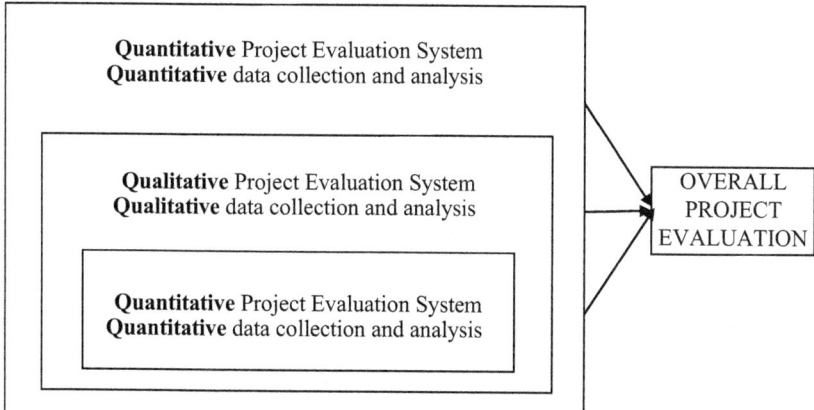

Fig. 6.6 Hybrid mixed systems. (Source: Based on Creswell and Plano Clark (2010))

most commonly used. The author also usually focuses his research on this type of mixed system for project evaluation.

An important complement to the parallel and sequential mixed systems is the hybrid mixed system (triangulation multi-level design), the general scheme of which is shown in Fig. 6.6. In this multi-level design, various methods are used in different system levels (Tashakkori and Teddlie 1998). In such hybrid mixed systems, different types of system may be used: quantitative and qualitative as well as classical and intelligent.

An example of the design of the mixed intelligent system for comprehensive project evaluation based on triangulation design (convergent parallel mixed systems) and hybrid mixed systems is shown in Fig. 6.7.

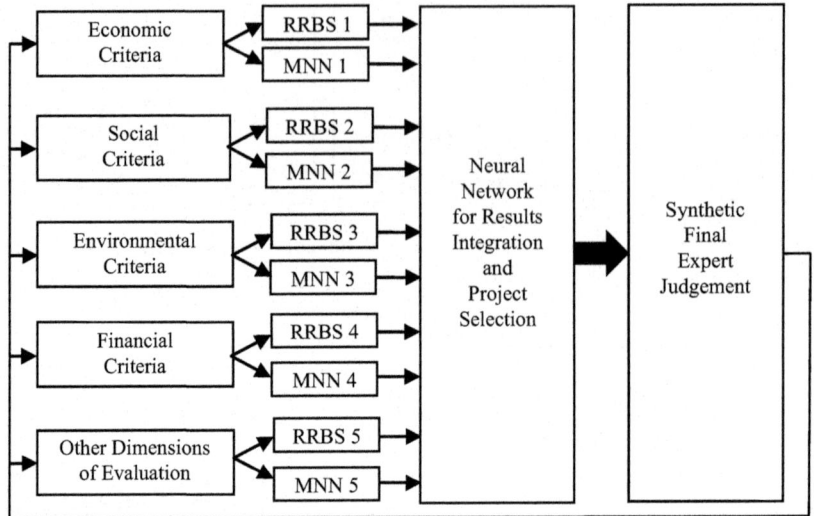

Fig. 6.7 Design of the mixed intelligent system for comprehensive project evaluation

This mixed intelligent system uses the parallel application of two intelligent systems: a rule-based system and neural networks. As a basis for the rule-based system, rough set theory (Grzeszczyk 2006) was proposed and therefore the term 'rough rule-based system' (RRBS) can be used. The data processed in RRBS reflects the opinions of experts and stakeholders, so they are descriptive and qualitative. The other predicted mixed intelligent system uses neural networks (MNN). Its task is to process quantitative data, complementing the qualitative data processed by RRBS.

For both RRBS and MNN systems, hybrid solutions based on the additional use of genetic algorithms are also used. In the first RRBS, this algorithm is used for supporting the learning process, and in the second system, with the support of results obtained from a genetic algorithm, neural network selection is performed.

The evaluation processes include economic, social, environmental, financial and other aspects. Individual aspects are considered as a result of running calculations in parallel modes (qualitative and quantitative) using RRBS and MNN systems. The different aspects of evaluation are of greater or lesser importance for different types of projects and should be selected accordingly. For example, for ordinary commercial projects implemented by

Fig. 6.8 Mixed intelligent system based on rough set decision rules

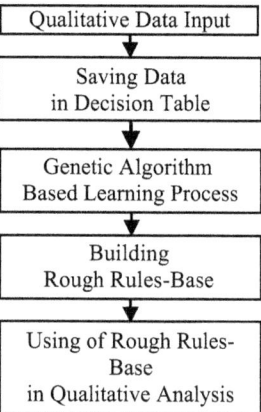

the private sector, financial evaluation is the most important. In practice, for these types of projects, the other aspects and dimensions are often skipped. The situation is different in the case of public projects, for which economic, social, environmental and other aspects are the most important.

Figure 6.8 shows an outline of the design of RRBS—the mixed intelligent system based on rough set decision rules. This kind of qualitative intelligent classification system can use empirical qualitative data about evaluated projects from project evaluation experts. These empirical data are collected in decision tables, which are a typical way to record initial knowledge of evaluated objects when using rough set theory. In the next steps, activities related to generate decision rules and building a rough rules base are performed. Generation of decision-making rules takes place as a result of system learning. The built rough rules base can then be used in project classification processes realization (Grzeszczyk 2017).

Figure 6.9 shows how mixed intelligent systems use neural networks (MNN). Quantitative data is entered at the input of this system. The next step is to select the architectures and types of neural networks, with the support of genetic algorithm calculations. Selected neural networks are then subject to learning processes. The quality of neural networks built and learned is evaluated and improved. If satisfactory network improvement parameters are achieved, they are used in quantitative analysis.

At the end of the complete and comprehensive evaluation process, in accordance with the proposed model, a multi-stakeholder team should be involved in the collective and synthetic final expert judgment.

Fig. 6.9 Mixed intelligent system based on neural networks

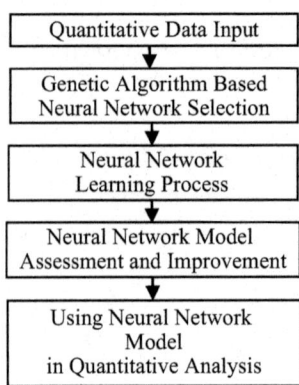

On the one hand, the use of mixed intelligent systems can potentially be a source of satisfaction for evaluators, implementing research processes that are interesting and scientifically valuable. On the other hand, there are many problems that can arise as a result of combining systems that are frequently different: quantitative and qualitative as well as classical and intelligent.

The integration of quantitative and qualitative methods and systems is accompanied by the following problems (Johnson and Onwuegbuzie 2004).

1. It is often necessary to establish research teams due to the lack of sufficiently comprehensive qualifications in individual researchers.
2. Notwithstanding the need to engage significant intellectual capital resources of evaluators, mixed research processes are usually expensive and time-consuming.
3. Some question the meaning of mixed-methodological paradigms and suggest that only one of the two paradigms—quantitative or qualitative—should be used.
4. In particular, when using the sequential coupled system, there are often problems with quantization of qualitative data, or converting unstructured data to structured form.

It is worth considering carefully whether in certain situations there is really a need to overcome these problems, incur considerable costs and carry out more complicated and time-consuming mixed research processes, compared to research based on individual methods and systems. In the case of mixed intelligent systems designs, considerable difficulties connected with the combination of quantitative and qualitative systems are further compounded by complex and relatively unknown intelligent systems.

6.5   DEVELOPMENT OF EVALUATION SYSTEMS

The problems of evaluation of the activities undertaken have been perceived for years in the theory and practice of business and management sciences, as well as in project management, which is a separate field. Methods and evaluation systems are being developed that may contribute to reducing the multifaceted risk of unique and complex activities undertaken under various types of projects. Contemporary research related to evaluation systems refers to historical achievements in the field of evaluation.

Attempts are being made to create presentations of summaries and the historical development of project evaluation. One of these attempts identified the following seven significant time periods (seen from the US perspective) (Hogan 2007).

1. The Age of Reform. The first formal use of evaluation was in 1792 (the use of quantitative measures to evaluate students' performance), then in 1897 the first evaluation of an educational program in the US was carried out.

2. The Period of Efficiency and Testing. At the beginning of the twentieth century, the achievements of Fredrick W. Taylor on scientific management and efficiency became the inspiration for administrators in education in the field of measurement and evaluation (summarizing student test performance and grading).

3. The Tylerian Age. In the years 1930–1945, Ralph Tyler initiated and developed educational evaluation research.

4. The Period of Innocence. In the early years after World War II, properly evaluating educational programs was not considered sufficiently important, but the Taxonomy of Educational Objectives was developed, which was the basis for further development of evaluation in education.

5. The Age of Development. During the Cold War, research was funded on evaluation systems for measuring the success of educational development projects in technical sciences, mathematics and foreign languages. In the early 1960s, criterion-referenced testing began.

6. The Period of Professionalization. During the 1970s evaluation became a profession; the publication of a number of journals dedicated to this field began and universities started to teach students on evaluation methodology courses.

7. The Phase of Expansion and Integration. After a period of stagnation in the early 1980s, evaluation became more integrated in the 1990s and professional associations and evaluation standards developed. These development processes are still ongoing.

Contemporary evaluation methods and systems development result from a gradual departure from looking at business projects merely from the point of view of achieving short-term financial benefits. Increasingly, such projects are also evaluated taking into account additional aspects: social, environmental, economic, organizational, legal and others. Such an approach to the evaluation of business projects is often related to the strategic nature of evaluated projects or the pursuit of compliance with the sustainability concept.

Multifaceted evaluation is nothing new in the case of development, public and European projects. They are evaluated in this way in relation to their nature and the requirements imposed by the founders within the system of program documents.

The importance of public and development initiatives, projects and programs is steadily increasing, and along with this increase, extensive evaluation research is being developed. The results of these studies are often adapted to various types of organizations from the business sector, which implement more and more projects that require multi-criteria evaluation methods in addition to comprehensive evaluation systems and are not limited to basic financial analysis techniques.

Table 6.1 illustrates a kind of vision of the development of project evaluation methods and systems. The presentation of this vision can be started with the evaluation methods based on scientific management theory, according to which there are four basic functions: planning, organizing, leading and controlling. The following definition is related to these functions: project management is the planning, organizing, directing and controlling of organization's resources to achieve particular objectives expected by the project stakeholders in an effective and efficient manner (Kerzner 2009).

From the point of view of the aforementioned functions, contemporary project evaluation refers to the two functions of management and project management: planning (ex-ante evaluation aka appraisal of new projects) and control (ex-post evaluation aka final evaluation). At the beginning of the development of evaluation systems, more attention was paid to the criterion of efficiency (profitability) related to the maximization of financial outcomes and minimization of costs.

Table 6.1   Development of project evaluation methods and systems

Evaluation Methods and Systems	Evaluation Criteria	Principles
Methods based on scientific management and efficiency	Monetary approach: cost and price	Informal, not precisely described theory
Fragmentary evaluation methods regarding financial and quantitative aspects	Profitability approach: quantitative, financial, fragmentary, valued in monetary terms	Based on a well-known cash flow metrics
Multi-criteria evaluation systems	Complexity approach: quantitative, often conflicting criteria	Decision-making in complex environments
Comprehensive evaluation systems	Multidimensionality approach: monetary and non-monetary, quantitative and qualitative	Universal, formalized and comprehensive approaches
Intelligent evaluation systems	Quantitative or qualitative criteria in uncertainty conditions	AI, machine learning principles, biologically or mathematically inspired
Mixed Intelligent Systems	Multidimensionality, multifacetedness in uncertainty conditions	Systems approaches, Integral Theory, classical and AI based integrated approaches, methodological pluralism and triangulation, complex research design, the most complete and comprehensive evaluation problems understanding

Source: Based on Grzeszczyk (2016b)

For the continuation of the classical approach based on scientific management theory, research on basic financial analysis techniques and quantitative evaluation systems of financial efficiency of investment projects can be considered. For these systems, the costs and benefits are quantified in financial terms and simple financial indicators are used, for example, Present Value (PV), Net Present Value (NPV), Internal Rate of Return (IRR) and others. Such well-known cash flow-based metrics are used in the case of ordinary financial analysis of project efficiency, for outcomes evaluation, which is relatively easy to present in a financial form. If only financial benefits for entrepreneurs are taken into account, positive and negative social aspects and the impact of the project on the natural environment and other factors are not considered.

In the case of evaluation of development, public and European projects as well as strategic projects, it is not enough to apply fragmentary evaluation methods regarding only financial and quantitative aspects. It is necessary to use specific evaluation methods that take into account various non-monetary outcomes and impacts of projects, in addition to evaluation systems adapted to projects with multifaceted effects: solving multi-criteria decision-making problems should be used.

The natural direction of development of methods and systems concerning fragmented evaluation (referring to only one, selected aspect) is to conduct research on multifaceted and comprehensive evaluation systems. Therefore, attempts are being made to build models of such systems, for example, using mixed methods and mixed systems. More often, however, several narrowly specialized evaluation methods are used simultaneously within individual evaluation processes.

If one assumes that comprehensive evaluation should be understood as a multi-stage process (structuring evaluation process, data collection, analyzing evaluation data, interpretation and evaluating alternative solutions), narrowly specialized and fragmentary evaluation methods can be assigned to individual stages. A system of methods is in this case used for comprehensive evaluation, and in one evaluation process from several to a dozen different fragmentary methods can be used.

The last two stages of project evaluation systems development are related to undertaking interdisciplinary methodological studies that concern applications of intelligent systems in solving complex project evaluation problems. As part of this type of research, one can deal with the usefulness of individual intelligent systems and mixed intelligent systems, which are the subject of the considerations presented in this book.

Different authors undertake to determine emerging trends shaping future project evaluation status and such trends include, for example, the following (Worthen et al. 2004, Hogan 2007):

- increased importance of qualitative methods and preference for using multiple-method,
- a strong shift toward application of mixed methods and systems in each program evaluation,
- development of logic models and theory-based evaluation,
- increased application of advanced evaluation systems within organizations from private, public and nonprofit sectors,

- more and more advanced ICT technologies available to evaluators,
- increased application of evaluation to empower a project's stakeholders,
- increased importance of ethical issues in conducting project evaluation,
- increased priority of internal evaluation.

Due to the fact that in project evaluation processes the collection and analysis of quantitative as well as qualitative data, information and knowledge have fundamental importance, systems that ensure the correct implementation of these activities are becoming more and more significant. Therefore, new data and knowledge processing technologies, combined with intelligent data analytics methods and knowledge-based systems, are becoming of key importance for project evaluation systems. It is desirable to conduct research in this area and to look for new approaches, methods and systems inspired by progress in the field of advanced intelligent computational technologies.

There is also a need and the possibility of developing comprehensive evaluation based on mixed intelligent systems, and such research should have an interdisciplinary character. Studies of this kind are relevant and by meeting existing challenges they can also lead to the development of new models supporting multi-aspect project evaluation. Many modern IT approaches derived from data science enable the automation of complex evaluation processes, also increasing their objective character as well as following in the direction of knowledge-driven and data-driven evaluation.

References

Aarseth, W., Ahola, T., Aaltonen, K., Okland, A., & Andersen, B. (2017, August). Project Sustainability Strategies: A Systematic Literature Review. *International Journal of Project Management, 35*(6), 1071–1083.

Creswell, J. W. (2014). *Research Design: Qualitative, Quantitative and Mixed Methods Approaches*. California: SAGE Publications Inc. Thousand Oaks, California 91320.

Creswell, J. W., & Plano Clark, V. L. (2010). *Designing and Conducting Mixed Methods Research*. SAGE Publications Inc. Thousand Oaks, California 91320.

Grzeszczyk, T. A. (2006). Application of the Rough Set Method for Evaluation of Structural Funds Projects. In *ICEIS 2006. Proceedings of the Eighth International Conference on Enterprise Information Systems*. Paphos: Artificial Intelligence and Decision Support Systems.

Grzeszczyk, T. A. (2016a). Sustainable Project Evaluation. In T. A. Grzeszczyk (Ed.), *Selected Aspects of Sustainability in Project Management and Evaluation*. Warsaw: OW PW.

Grzeszczyk, T. A. (2016b). Development of Intelligent Models for Project Evaluation. In P. Bartkowiak & A. Jaki (Eds.), *Dilemmas of Management Sciences Development. Methodological Perspective*. Warsaw: Scientific Society for Organization and Management.

Grzeszczyk, T. A. (2017). *Rough Rule-Based Systems for Sparse and Dense Data Analysis Used in Project Evaluation* (Vol. 31). 4th International Conference on Management Science and Management Innovation. Advances in Economics, Business and Management Research.

Hogan, R. L. (2007). The Historical Development of Program Evaluation: Exploring the Past and Present. *Online Journal of Workforce Education and Development, II*(4), 1–14.

Johnson, R. B., & Onwuegbuzie, A. J. (2004, October). Mixed Methods Research: A Research Paradigm Whose Time Has Come. *Educational Researcher, 33*(7), 14–26.

Kerzner, H. (2009). *Project Management: A Systems Approach to Planning, Scheduling, and Controlling*. New Jersey: John Wiley & Sons.

Silvius, G. (2017). Sustainability as a New School of Thought in Project Management. *Journal of Cleaner Production, 166*(November), 1479–1493.

Tashakkori, A. M., & Teddlie, C. B. (1998). *Mixed Methodology: Combining Qualitative and Quantitative Approaches*. SAGE Publications Inc. Thousand Oaks, California 91320.

Wilber, K. (2003). Foreword. In F. Visser (Ed.), *Ken Wilber: Thought as Passion*. Albany: State University of New York Press.

Worthen, B. R., Sanders, J. R., & Fitzpatrick, J. L. (2004). *Educational Evaluation: Alternative Approaches and Practical Guidelines*. Boston: Allyn and Bacon.

CHAPTER 7

Summary

Abstract In the last chapter, the author methodically summarizes the results of study dedicated to mixed intelligent systems and the development of models for project management and evaluation. A summary of holistic reflections on the Multi-Level Evaluation Model, the Integral Multi-Level Evaluation Model and an example of design of a mixed intelligent system for comprehensive project evaluation is presented. The results obtained confirm the assumption from the research that it can be useful to integrate project evaluation models, applying both traditional methods and those based on intelligent systems. A possible direction for evaluation systems development is also identified.

Keywords Results of evaluation methods review • Holistic reflections • Interdisciplinary research conclusions

In this book, the author methodically summarizes the results of research dedicated to mixed intelligent systems and the development of models for project management and evaluation, which take into account the current state of knowledge in the field of project management based on business and management sciences. The research problem undertaken is the result of finding the need and opportunity to continue interdisciplinary research concerning the development of new models of comprehensive project evaluation systems.

© The Author(s) 2018
T. A. Grzeszczyk, *Mixed Intelligent Systems*,
https://doi.org/10.1007/978-3-319-91158-8_7

As a result of an approaches review of methods and techniques that can be used in evaluation systems and their development over the years, the inevitable necessity of moving away from classical concepts can be observed. In the past, within the evaluation processes of projects and programs, the knowledge and experience of evaluation experts were primarily used. The dynamic development of quantitative and qualitative methods to support decision-making within these processes contributed to the fact that it is difficult to imagine the planning and implementation of an evaluation without the help of more or less complex evaluation systems supported by IT technologies.

The studies are consistent with important contemporary mainstream research showing that the integration of several evaluation methods represents one of the alternative directions of project evaluation system development toward complex and comprehensive solutions. This type of study, related to the search for new models, contributing to the improvement of previously known evaluation systems and combining several methods is justified. The results obtained confirm the assumption from the research that it can be useful to integrate project evaluation models, applying both traditional evaluation methods and methods based on intelligent systems.

In this book, holistic reflections on the Multi-Level Evaluation Model, the Integral Multi-Level Evaluation Model and an example of design of a mixed intelligent system for comprehensive project evaluation are presented. The first model has several evaluation dimensions and four subsequent levels of project management and evaluation: projects, programs, project and program portfolios as well as the strategic organization level. The second model is an example of Integral Theory application that constitutes a kind of 'meta-paradigm' that allows for the combination of separate paradigms, approaches and systems into an interrelated framework for multifaceted project evaluation.

The presented example of design of a mixed intelligent system is based on a triangulation solution (convergent parallel mixed systems) and hybrid mixed systems. Both symbolic and non-symbolic intelligent systems are used in this design. This mixed intelligent system uses the parallel application of two intelligent systems: a rule-based system (symbolic knowledge representation) and neural networks (non-symbolic knowledge representation). As a basis for the rule-based system, rough set theory was proposed and therefore the term 'rough rule-based system' (RRBS) is used. The data processed in an RRBS reflects the opinions of experts and stakeholders, so they are descriptive and qualitative.

The other predicted mixed intelligent system uses neural networks (MNN). Its task is to process quantitative data, complementing the qualitative data processed by RRBS. The evaluation processes include economic, social, environmental, financial and other aspects. Individual aspects are considered as a result of running calculations in parallel modes (qualitative and quantitative) using RRBS and MNN systems.

For both RRBS and MNN systems, hybrid solutions based on the additional use of genetic algorithms are also applied. In the first, RRBS, this algorithm is used for supporting the learning process, and in the second system, with the support of results obtained thanks to a genetic algorithm, neural network selection is performed.

There is a need to conduct interdisciplinary research without conventional academic boundaries within models of mixed intelligent systems and various kinds of mixed design applications in solving complex project evaluation problems. The scientific reflections and general models presented in this book can be the basis for further activities related to the development of formalized mathematical models to implement proposed solutions and mixed intelligent systems for comprehensive project evaluation.

The proposed holistic approaches to solving a complex evaluation problem are characterized by a multi-aspect and interdisciplinary character. Within these approaches it is possible to take into account many quantitative and qualitative aspects as well as sustainability aspects. The universality of the developed models is expressed by the suitability for application within the evaluation processes of various types of projects, as well as the possibilities of applying them to various types of evaluation: ex-ante, ongoing and ex-post.

The obtained results of interdisciplinary research may be useful for experts for different project evaluations, project managers, business professionals, academics and students—the future experts for preparing, implementing and evaluating projects.

Interdisciplinary methodological studies in the field of project evaluation play an increasing role in the management sciences in connection with the rising difficulties of collection and processing of growing data sets. Evaluators should pay attention to Big Data technologies and seek new methods and mixed intelligent systems whose creation is possible because of the development of new IT technologies. Thanks to solutions based, among other factors, on achievements in AI and knowledge engineering, the range of potential methods and systems that can be used in comprehensive mixed intelligent systems can be significantly expanded.

One of the possible directions of evaluation systems development is not only progress in research on mixed intelligent systems but also the use of ever newer knowledge systems, AI technology and Big Data analytics. Further development of intelligent and mixed evaluation systems may even lead to reducing the role of expert evaluators in favor of systems based on knowledge and deep learning. In project evaluation processes, expert panels will be increasingly replaced by two parallel knowledge discovery modeling mechanisms: data-driven, based on data mining, and knowledge-driven, based on human expert knowledge.

INDEX

© The Author(s) 2018
T. A. Grzeszczyk, *Mixed Intelligent Systems*,
https://doi.org/10.1007/978-3-319-91158-8

Printed by Printforce, the Netherlands